Challenging Cryptograms

Helen Nash

 Sterling Publishing Co., Inc. New York

For my mother, Dorothy Searles, who gave me a love of cryptograms, and for my husband, Dave, who did everything but windows so that I might play with these puzzles.

I thank Hannah Steinmetz, editor extraordinaire, whose warm support and creative intelligence turned a collection into a book.

Library of Congress Cataloging-in-Publication Data

Nash, Helen, 1944-
    Challenging cryptograms / by Helen Nash.
       p. cm.
    ISBN 0-8069-0594-8
    1. Cryptograms. I. Title.
  GV1507.C8N37 1994   93-39591
  793.73--dc20   CIP

10 9 8 7 6 5 4 3 2 1

Published by Sterling Publishing Company, Inc.
387 Park Avenue South, New York, N.Y. 10016
© 1994 by Helen Nash
Distributed in Canada by Sterling Publishing
c/o Canadian Manda Group, P.O.Box 920, Station U
Toronto, Ontario, Canada M8Z 5P9
Distributed in Great Britain and Europe by Cassell PLC
Villiers House, 41/47 Strand, London WC2N 5JE, England
Distributed in Australia by Capricorn Link (Australia) Pty Ltd.
P.O. Box 6651, Baulkham Hills, Business Centre, NSW 2153, Australia
Manufactured in the United States of America
All rights reserved

Sterling ISBN 0-8069-0594-8

Contents

Introduction

This book came about because I am hopelessly addicted to cryptograms. The single offering in the morning paper could not satisfy my appetite. And like many other cryptogram addicts, I awakened some mornings with my brain snoozing on the feather pillow down the hall. There have been mornings when no amount of coffee could spark my brain into action. Instead of "My kingdom for a horse," I found myself muttering, "My kingdom for a clue—or two."

While this collection of puzzles is perfect for beginners, I think of it as the answer to the "morning fuzzies." Whichever you might be, expert, beginner, or brain-befuddled, this book can satisfy. Solve the puzzles without peeking at the clues. Fudge a little and use Clue One. Or pour yourself another cup of coffee and peek at Clue Two. Whatever, this collection of witty and humorous crypto-quips is sure to make you smile.

Enjoy!

Helen Nash

How to Use This Book

This book is organized into four sections:

1. The cryptograms: Witty or humorous quotations along with their authors' names, author and book, or character and television program or film. These are converted into puzzles with each letter of the alphabet standing for another. Although each quote has its own code, within that quote the same letter will represent its corresponding letter throughout.

2. Clue One: A separate section at the end of the cryptogram collection in which one clue, or letter equivalent, is offered for each puzzle. Since each puzzle has its own code, each puzzle will have a different clue offering. Clue One gives the brain a start, but it won't make the puzzle too easy to solve.

3. Clue Two: A separate section following the Clue One section, in which a second letter equivalent is given for each puzzle. Clue Two offers a hint that alone, or with the first clue, will lead the brain toward the solution.

4. Solutions: The decoded quotations for each puzzle.

Hints for Solving Cryptograms

1. Single-letter words will be "I" or "a."

2. Frequent use of the same three-letter word may indicate the word "the." Notice that the word "he" is part of the word "the."

3. An apostrophe is usually followed by "t" as in contractions (don't) or by "s" as in possessives (dog's tail). Remember that a word ending with an apostrophe is probably a plural noun ending in "s." An apostrophe at the beginning of a word indicates the initial letters have been dropped, like the "th" in the word "them."

4. A question mark at the end of a quotation tells you the first word is likely who, what, when, where, how, or why.

5. Certain consonants occur together, such as "th," "wh," "sh," and "ch."

6. Likewise, the position of letters at the end of a word may indicate common endings such as "-tion", "-ent," or "-ant," "-ing," or "-ed."

7. Short, single-syllable words that have "-ed" or "-ing" added to them double their final consonant, such as in "beginning" or "hopped."

8. In a two-letter word, one letter must be a vowel.

9. Often the author's name can be figured out, thereby leading to more clues within the quotation itself.

10. If you reach an impasse, read the puzzle and let your mind fill in the blanks. The English language is based upon the basic structure of who is doing what, with descriptive or qualifying phrases rounding out the picture.

Cryptograms

1. SUXQ SX HDOG HB MBR, SX'JX
   (WHEN WE TALK TO GOD, WE'RE)
   NJDCFQM. SUXQ MBR HDOGW HB LW,
   (PRAYING. WHEN GOD TALKS TO US,)
   SX'JX WYUFPBNUJXQFY.
   (WE'RE SCHIZOPHRENIC)
   —IDQX SDMQXJ
   (JANE WAGNER)

2. EFCR CR L NJYY XMAKEJI. NMWOR
   (THIS IS A FREE COUNTRY FOLKS)
   FLQY L JCSFE EM RYKB UY WYEEYJR,
   (HAVE A RIGHT TO SEND ME LETTERS)
   LKB C FLQY L JCSFE KME EM JYLB
   (AND I HAVE A RIGHT NOT TO READ)
   EFYU. —ZCWWCLU NLAWOKYJ
   (THEM WILLIAM FAULKNER)

3. HDNDB MHNDTK WGPB FGHDW MH
   (NEVER INVEST YOUR MONEY IN)
   XHWKUMHR KUXK DXKT GB HDDQT
   (ANYTHING THAT EATS OR NEEDS)
   BDOXMBMHR. —LMVVW BGTD
   (REPAIRING BILLY ROSE)

4. UAIZ XDZ XUUXDRFCXZ MC UTX UE
   (ONCE THE TOOTHPASTE IS OUT OF)
   XDZ XTOZ, MX'C DFSG XU NZX MX
   (THE TUBE, IT'S HARD TO GET IT)
   OFIB MA. —D.S. DFJGZLFA
   (BACK IN H. R. HALDEMAN)

5. PTK DFXXKHP HKBBKO FH YJJLDJJLH
   (THE BIGGEST SELLER IS COOKBOOKS)
   QUA PTK HKYJUA FH AFKP DJJLH—TJM
   (AND THE SECOND IS DIET BOOKS HOW)
   UJP PJ KQP MTQP GJS'NK VSHP BKQOUKA
   (NOT TO EAT WHAT YOU'RE JUST LEARNED)
   TJM PJ YJJL. —QUAG OJJUKG
   (HOW TO COOK ANDY ROONEY)

6. THERE IS NO DILEMMA COMPARED WITH THAT OF THE DEEP SEA DIVER WHO HEARS THE MESSAGE FROM THE SHIP ABOVE, COME UP AT ONCE WE ARE SINKING. —ROBERT COOPER

6. OTUXU LP CW SLMUKKQ RWKYQXUS BLOT OTQO WH OTU SUUY-PUQ SLIUX BTW TUQXP OTU KUPPQDU HXWK OTU PTLY QAWIU, "RWKU JY QO WCRU. BU QXU PLCGLCD." —XWAUXO RWWYUX

7. AGE IS STRICTLY A CASE OF MIND OVER MATTER. IF YOU DON'T MIND IT DOESN'T MATTER. —JACK BENNY

7. BDZ EK KLPEYLSI B YBKZ QX NETA QOZP NBLLZP. EX IQF AQT'L NETA, EL AQZKT'L NBLLZP. —CBYV UZTTI

8. THE REAL MENACE IN DEALING WITH A FIVE YEAR OLD IS THAT IN NO TIME AT ALL YOU BEGIN TO SOUND LIKE A FIVE YEAR OLD —JEAN KERR

8. VIL ULBM JLRBYL QR ALBMQRX FQVI B CQOL-HLBU-ZMA QD VIBV QR RZ VQJL BV BMM HZG KLXQR VZ DZGRA MQWL B CQOL-HLBU-ZMA. —SLBR WLUU

9. MANY A MAN OWES HIS SUCCESS TO HIS FIRST WIFE AND HIS SECOND TO HIS SUCCESS —JIM BACKUS

9. GIAO I GIA KEQY MCY YPVVQYY LK MCY NCDYL ECNQ IAJ MCY YQVKAJ LK MCY YPVVQYY. —FCG HIVTPY

10. IT'S NO LONGER A QUESTION OF STAYING HEALTHY. IT'S A QUESTION OF FINDING A SICKNESS YOU LIKE. —JACKIE MASON

10. PX'U KI NIKFGZ M BJGUXPIK IA UXMVPKF OGMNXOV. PX'U M BJGUXPIK IA APKQPKF M UPTHKGUU VIJ NPHG. —LMTHPG EMUIK

11. O GWIB W QONEKFWIB AOEBJHWNB.

I HAVE A MICROWAVE FIREPLACE

XKS NWR HWX ZKFR OR AEKRY KA YGB

YOU CAN LAY DOWN IN FRONT OF THE

AOEB WHH ROUGY OR BOUGY QORSYBD.

FIRE ALL NIGHT IN EIGHT MINUTES

       —DYBJGBR FEOUGY

—STEPHEN WRIGHT

12. TJZ BHW KJD NL LASLBOLF OJ

HOW CAN YOU BE EXPECTED TO

UJMLIW H BJDWOIK OTHO THY OZJ

GOVERN A COUNTRY THAT HAS TWO

TDWFILF PJIOK-YQA RQWFY JP

HUNDRED FORTY SIX KINDS OF

BTLLYL?   —BTHICLY FL UHDCCL

CHEESE   *CHARLES DE GAULLE*

13. OBGH LBG VACFGHK DX LBG

WHEN THE BURDENS OF THE

YCGKEFGHWS KGGP AHAKAUJJS

PRESIDENCY SEEM UNUSUALLY

BGUZS, E UJOUSK CGPEHF PSKGJX EL

HEAVY, I ALWAYS REMIND MYSELF IT

WDAJF VG ODCKG. E WDAJF VG U

COULD BE WORSE. I COULD BE A

PUSDC.   —JSHFDH V. QDBHKDH

MAYOR   *LYNDON B JOHNSON*

14. QL RME'H FUKL UEW

WE DON'T HAVE ANY

VLGVTBLVUHMVA. QL FUKL U GLQ

REFRIGERATORS. WE HAVE A FEW

SMHOLNNW AHMKLA, OCH HFLW'VL ME

POTBELLY STOVES, BUT THEY'RE ON

HFL PMUPFTEB AHUGG.

THE COACHING STAFF

      —PMUPF RUKL PCVVW

COACH DAVE CURRY

15. *DISNEY OF COURSE HAS THE*
BXJIZR, VQ YVWSJZ, GPJ AGZ
BEST CASTING. IF HE DOESN'T LIKE
CZJA YPJAXIM. XQ GZ BVZJI'A OXNZ
AN ACTOR HE JUST TEARS HIM UP
PI PYAVS, GZ FWJA AZPSJ GXK WT.
ALFRED HITCHCOCK
—POQSZB GXAYGYVYN

16. *HAVING A FAMILY IS LIKE*
PWRDUS W EWFDAZ DQ ADJK
HAVING A BOWLING ALLEY
PWRDUS W HNBADUS WAAKZ
INSTALLED IN YOUR BRAIN
DUQVWAAKI DU ZNTM HMWDU.
MARTIN MULL
—FWMVDU FTAA

17. *THERE ARE NO SICK PEOPLE IN*
QTVXV IXV KU RDJF AVUAZV DK
NORTH OXFORD. THEY ARE EITHER
KUXQT ULMUXG. QTVH IXV VDQTVX
DEAD OR ALIVE. IT'S SOMETIMES
GVIG UX IZDWV. DQ'R RUBVQDBVR
DIFFICULT TO TELL THE
GDMMDJNZQ QU QVZZ QTV
DIFFERENCE, THAT'S ALL
GDMMVXVKJV, QTIQ'R IZZ.
BARBARA PYM
—EIXEIXI AHB

18. *WHEN A MAN OF FORTY FALLS IN*
CDSV P FPV UI IUEXZ IPOOK BV
LOVE WITH A GIRL OF TWENTY, IT
OUHS CBXD P MBEO UI XCSVXZ, BX
ISN'T HER YOUTH HE IS SEEKING
BKV'X DSE ZUWXD DS BK KSSJBVM
BUT HIS OWN. *LENORE COFFEE*
RWX DBK UCV. —OSVUES TUIISS

19. UVJ ZOJGU IPOOQLUJO PX LQDBSI

KGA SF UVJ JZP...BPPTSAZ GU UVJ

KSOOPO MSFUOGIUF PAJ'F GUUJAUSPA

XOPK UVJ LOPDBJK.   —MJGA GIVJFPA

20. VXCGTVU TM TLIXMMTKDJ PXW

CGJ LFV AGX EXJMV'C GFQJ CX EX TC

GTLMJDP.   —FVXVBLXRM

21. CE GHKFXRKAD FU ZAGDKAD GZ

ZPAL JLRJ GU RKEFKD CDKJGFKDW

AFQQDX KGJXRJD, G ZLFPNW JLGKT

LD IRZ JRNTGKH RSFPJ QFNGADCDK'Z

FODXJGCD.

        —RXALSGZLFQ UXDWDXGAT

        WFKRNW AFHHRK

22. SXIXJ UJZSD ATYBD BKVVXX YH

TPSBN; ZH FZTT DXXC LKP YFYDX ZS

HNX YVHXJSKKS.   —MZTTL BKKCXJ

23. GHNIG FTIG KZ EKCRDKGA I NHC
PJCCJF GHS CDIC DJ DIZ DKZ RWFXJ PINN
ZCFIKADCJGJM HWC.   —QHJ AIFIAKHNI

24. LVQ BG MAV ATGYL HX INZEBW
VYNWTMHKL BL GHM T IKVMMR MABGU.
                        —DVOBG TKGHEY,
                  "MAV PHGYVK RVTKL"

25. DICCZVD RZERIL BSC BJ COI
XHIPZEXV KXP XGGBEZXCZBV ZG YZRI
DICCZVD RZERIL BSC BJ COI KBBR-
BJ-COI-HBVCO EYSK.   —HIYWZV KIYYZ

26. LKXB QEB QORPQ DLBP LRQ LC Y
OBIYQFLKPEFM, FQ'P OBYIIV KL CRK
IVFKD QL 'BJ YKVJLOB.
           —KLOJ MBQBOPLK, "XEBBOP"

27. RWHRZP YININXIY BTRB HI MRPP
BTOP HRZ XAB KLJI. ALWIPP ZKAY
PMKAPI OP YIRUOLV BTI YKRU NRM.
                        —YKXIYB KYXIL

12

28. OQ ETZ XESTQ, PEIOUH, IZ IZUZ

PBTQZUN OTH MOQPZUZUN OTH QPZT

NZZJN ASCZ OAA EG O NBHHZT IZ

WZKOJZ XOUQLMEZUN.   —ROTZ IOMTZU

29. VJR BRTOEOYV TWXRTREV JDY

JRMZRF WZRE TOEFY DEF IOVKJREY

VW VJR EWVOWE VJDV TRE KDE LR DV

JWTR WE VJR PDEUR.   —PRER XRDCQ

30. FGEVDVPX: DKT HTMDET ZOD GI

HTDDVMH NGDTX IOGW DKT FGGO ZMS

PZWFZVHM IRMSX IOGW DKT OVPK, JQ

FOGWVXVMH DG FOGDTPD TZPK IOGW

DKT GDKTO.   —ZMGMQWGRX

31. K YHUHVKCFKQ FO K JHCOTQ XET

XTQ'V HKV KQZVEFQU VEKV IKQ EKYH

IEFDLCHQ.   —LKYFL PCHQQHC

32. SOKDU S MDSU ZH KCDUSBM, YM

BQMACZSKUZQK QSZE KT YD, "YSMVD GZOD

ZQH'K OTU DJDUMTHD."

                          —GSUUM VUTNH

13

33. RFC ACSTCR DK ARBLZQV LDWQV
ZA RD XZPC FDQCARXL, CBR AXDIXL,
BQY XZC BJDWR LDWT BVC.

       —XWSZXXC JBXX

34. OBUSU YA J EYDU NYEEUSUDPU
WE RUSARUPOYKU CUOQUUD LUOOYDL
YDKWVKUN JDN CUYDL PWXXYOOUN.
YD BJX JDN ULLA, OBU PBYPZUD YA
YDKWVKUN, CHO OBU RYL YA
PWXXYOOUN. —GWBD-JVVUD RSYPU

35. Q YXSQOH E VBL BI NZ QSBUQUW QU
LKO YEGJ ZESH.   —FKZVVQT HQVVOS

36. Q TCRZHWQV CB Q RKFBHG XYH OQG
VKZZ LHJ VH UH VH YKZZ CG BJOY Q XQL
VYQV LHJ QOVJQZZL ZHHA EHFXQFT VH
VYK VFCR.   —OQBBCK BVCGGKVV

37. OH'P YSH HLBH O'Z BCKBOF HS
FOA. O NDPH FSY'H RBYH HS IA HLAKA
RLAY OH LBMMAYP. —RSSFE BQQAY

38. XC JXK XC B'Q GHDGFKDFZ, AYF
HDUM KFXCHD JHK GHHRBDE BC AH
RFFV MHNK YXDZC WNCM TYBUF MHN
AYBDR XWHNA CHQFAYBDE FUCF.

                          —CNF EKXJAHD

39. PHWA, HV RX ACBHRKBHUV, HC K
QHUPUFHTKP RHCKEDAVBMJA BOKB YA
BAJRHVKBA UV BOA COUMPEAJC UW
CHZ CBJKVFA RAV YOUCA UVPX
UQNATBHDA HC BU RKIA K OUPA HV
UVA YHBO XUM.   —WJAE KPPAV

40. IUP FDQ GTPOG D FTIOGDV MDVV
DMUPG DO YDT DO IUP FDQ GLTUJ
XG.   —YDXGL SUSFUTQ

41. DHIDZH JAFS SIUITOTM OJOTPN
OTH ZIIYHP BDIU JAFS PANROWIT.
JIBZP MIB ZHF OU SIUITOTM
XHKSOUAK RAG MIBT QTOUP-UHJ
XHTKHPHN?   —UHAZ NAXIU

15

42. CE KUL WMUUV H BCBN, WMULJP

KUL LWN H WCJNQINA?

—WVNFMNQ RACZMV

43. NIYQ S'D WRUQY, S XWQ ARYYH

XTUAANWOA SQ GYJ NSCIUZC WQ

WTFZDYQC.   —MAW MAW FWGUT

44. SYV BNX UKSY HKW QKLH UKPP

NPUNEH JV YNCCKVA SYNX SYV BNX

UKSY HKW BKPPKGX LGPPNAH, JVRNIHV

SYV BNX UKSY HKW BKPPKGX LGPPNAH

NPUNEH UNXSH BGAV.   —NXGXEBGIH

45. OY O EVS VL GVTR VYYVOBL VL

PEXR LVR, O ZHJIS THZ AX LQXVFOTU

PH RHJ YBHG OTLOSX V CVB VP PEX

EVBKVBS GXSODVI LDEHHI.

—YBVTF LOTVPBV

46. KLM QDU LMP QDDG RDDNK VPDZ

LMP VEULMP. LM'K E XREKUHY

KCPQMDW.   —QPDCYLD ZEPS

16

47. IBH EBSPIHEI GTEIDZYH CHIMHHZ

IMS ASTZIE TE NZGHP YSZEIPNYITSZ.

—ZSHFTH DFTSIS

48. ZVCKPPZXKVWK ZT MQKV ESO

YZVH R JZTCRBK ZV ESOA ISTT'T

MSAB. MZTHSJ ZT MQKV ESO CQZVB

RISOC ZC RVH HKWZHK VSC CS

JKVCZSV ZC.   —RVSVEJSOT

49. VN WGN WSS MUGJ PLWGODJA,

QGNHL, WJZ HKUJIWJNUFH WJZ OFHI

MN PDXDSDYNZ MNQUGN VN WGN QDI

IU KWGIDPDKWIN DJ HUPDNIE.

—TFZDIL OWGIDJ

50. B CUFG PZ HUKVLM, TKL TGBDJ

YIEDJ UBD'L EDG EH LCGP.

—ABPPZ CEHHU

51. KBG KAHKB TNGY MNK RBOMIG

ORRNATLMI KN NHA OPLJLKZ KN

YKNSORB LK GSNKLNMOJJZ.

—UJOMMGAZ N'RNMMNA
17

52. MPSA LDB D MNK BPXZMAG LQAR
LQDK LA QNRNGAU LDB SDKQAG DRU
XNKQAG GDKQAG KQDR DMM XDVNG
FGAUPK FDGUB.   —GNCAGK NGCAR

53. R'W MRQOT JS UZZ MXRH
DJDHODHO UAJKM AOUKMB AORDN
JDZB HFRD-TOOI. MXUM'H TOOI
ODJKNX. YXUM TJ BJK YUDM, UD
UTJQUAZO IUDPQOUH?   —LOUD FOQQ

54. JTH JM KBH KBRTZV R'YH
SRVAJYHFHS RT ZHTHFGO GNJWK
FGRVRTZ URSV RV KBGK KBHL FHGOOL
SJT'K ZRYH G SGXT RM LJW QGOUHS
MRYH XROHV KJ VABJJO. —CGKKL SWUH

55. RMT RJGHUZT OVRM FGCT OGCTY
VF RMDR RMTI STR DZZ TKQVRTA DUGHR
YGRMVYS DYA RMTY CDJJI MVC.   —QMTJ

56. F SFZTJA FS MFZM MAAYQ OAJA
QV OVWRAJSTY, HAW OVTYR GA
OADJFWZ UMAH.   —QTA ZJDSUVW

57. XT CEIJ QKJE QZZXUYDJI SQFFYD
MXJSXD TXLY CXBYI ET SECY, MSO
UED'J MY CELY JYD CXBYI QMQO?

—CXZSQYB UQLXI

58. REZ HN YEGZ IKAA DY YEG VQPE
ENQV REGX XNYEDXF LNUGP?

—LNVB, "LNVB KXH LDXHZ"

59. LQDLXQ YCQ HCDYN-UOVNQN.
WKQJ'XX YTTQLW WKQ PYTW WKYW Y
LQCBDV TYV HQ YV YXTDKDXOT, Y
NDLQ POQVN, Y SOPQ HQYWQC YVN
QMQV Y VQSBLYLQCUYV, HGW OP Y
UYV NDQBV'W NCOMQ, WKQCQ'B
BDUQWKOVA SCDVA SOWK KOU.

—YCW HGTKSYXN

60. MBH MBAEC MBVM ADWOHNNHN DH
DPNM VUPFM VDHOATV AN MBH KVZ
WVOHEMN PUHZ MBHAO TBAQGOHE.

—HGKVOG, GFRH PJ KAEGNPO

61. RZ MLE XB BZ ILM XA KLR'A IF
YXDFM SXAO L RLG.   —KLCCXF BRZS

62. DPS VFWOJ OE WJ IFQWJ DPWD
EDWFDE AIFMOJQ DPS KIKSJD ZIC
QSD CH OJ DPS KIFJOJQ WJT TISE JID
EDIH CJDOX ZIC QSD OJDI DPS
IRROUS.   —FIVSFD RFIED

63. V RZKX OF NMFUPXG BVLR LRX
MVYR, FOPA BVLR LRFDX BRF RZKX Z
NMFUPXG UXVOW MVYR.

                    —TZKVT UMFBO

64. KDFB SBZL KN WZ R CNJZQPHZPK
NX VDZVMB RPL WRYRPVZB. PNT FK'B
RYY VDZVMB RPL PN WRYRPVZB.

                    —CQRVFZ RYYZP

65. CBKHKTKQ J'R NOIKM CBNE IJHM
GA CQJEJHX JO EBK RGOE
WSVQNEJTK, J BNTK EG ONP, QNHOGR
HGEKO.   —B.H. OCNHOGH

20

66. T YEVC VPG T LPCD YSADG, FEC
TC'V CLD QPIU SZ TC T LPCD YSVC.

                    —UPCLDHTAD YPAVZTDQN

67. NA DBAA NDSOBQN, DM THNW BA
GH LOBCT ISNQS GH GZS RHOWF NCF
GZSC GH TSG DM HRC NINOGDSCG.

                              —YNM WSCH

68. JT NRQ ECWH MR GHCOZ JM TORS
C XHGT-EHGU ARRI, NRQ SCN AH
AHNRZB EHGU.   —LHX XSJME

69. GOVM K GTC SWBM, K GTC CW
CEBLBKCVR K UWEZRM'D DTZX QWB T
IVTB TMR T OTZQ.   —PBTUKV TZZVM

70. IBMTM QN YR FEMNIQRY IBKI
TEHKYQKY-AMGQNB URRO QN BMKJL...
RYM HMKX QN MFEKX QY BMKJQYMNN,
Q GREXO WEMNN, IR MQWBI RT YQYM
LMKTN RU NIMKOL HEYW-ZMKY
MKIQYW.   —VKXJQY ITQXXQY

21

71. YVB COHM YZGB N DCGNO UBNHHM

RQTTBBPR ZO TVNOKZOK N GNO ZR

DVBO VB'R N ANAM. —ONYNHZB DCCP

72. KQPQYCICDO JTI UDOQ NVRJ GDL

EIWRJCTKLW SW IELQTUCOH

COGDLNTKCDO TSDVK CK, TI FQPP TI

RDOKLCSVKCOH KD KJQ OQQU GDL CK

—TPGLQU JCKRJRDRA

73. XACEX CEIA K VSFGMHKMOGI

BCILASI K WCVI CV ILG VSMGVI BKT

IA DST GUGMTILCEX DSI BLKI TAS

BGEI CE YAM CE ILG YCMVI FWKQG.

—LGWGE EKVL

74. ZUK SQL PRUXPKD U BQNMJ BPOYQLO

RDK? KQ ZNPRD UKJ MQOF QH YUEES

HUO BQRDK —RUNPQK FRPOY

75. OY'J BII IQUY B TYSRDBDQPV KPT

CYVVTPNQDL BVJ OY'J BII IQUY DP

HRL QD ZXYBS. —FQCVPV FZIBRCXIQV

76. ZVBVM TVZR ENHM XDM KN DZENZV
KN FCNQ ENH CDBV ISBVZ JSMKC.

— VMQD JNQJVXW

77. PR TK RPZ HC WQK RKTKY, HJ
ZBS'YK CBW AYKAPYKM WB IB PEE
WQK TPZ, MBC'W ASW ZBSY OBBWR BC
HC WQK JHYRW AEPNK.

— KM CBYWBC,

"WQK QBCKZDBBCKYR"

78. ELDMD PHRE JD PWMD EW ACVD
ELQG ZHRE DQECGX QGF XDEECGX
JCXXDM.   — EMCGQ YQHAHR

79. F BTUFDA ANVK F CPSADVA AVFXCK, F
WDFHV GFS TSOR TSBV... WPX XCVS,
TSBV NK VSTPLC, NKS'X NX?

— QPALV CFDDR KXTSV, "SNLCX BTPDX"

80. YO CAKZGMGLU EKAK M NHHX,
VPKU EHSRF LSV VPK RMJV VEH
LPMCVKAJ.   — GHAM KCPAHG

23

81. REO WLUO FLHV BU REO LSVX LSO
B'TO OTOW UOOS REIR B NBNS'R EITO
RL MVOIS.   —OWPI FLPFOMY

82. E ZYN YIZYSN WYJUAW WV
HRNTRXW GS RILRHN YOL E'KR OVZ
HRYXARL WAR YUR ZARO E LVO'W
AYKR YOSDVLS WV HRNTRXW.

                    —URVHUR DJHON

83. RSC SPVNO P YOZUCL GB ZQQ
SPVNO BQZUPSV BRFCI HPON OZIRO
EZILY. P VRO Z DGQQ NRGYC ZSL
DRGI BCRBQC LPCL.

                    —YOCBNCS HIPVNO

84. QBA LXXU NFPN KAQ ETZX P
KTDPOOX LXXUV VNDXR NFDBPN.

                    —PLL EPLUXDV

85. GM G JGJF'L YLHZL DHGFLGFX, G
BVOSJ EHNA ZHGYAJ KEGKUAFY.

                    —XZHFJIH IVYAY

86. BW QJWMDKNAO YAO K QDJHN VS.
RN XYAUNO UJ LNU BYDDKNO, YAO K
OKOA'U XYAU RKB UJ. —DKUY DVOAND

87. TUZNQ FBQ UCMHQW FE
MQSQLFAPQ MQWPALQ AM FE MFUWF
QPQWZECQ ERR AC FBQ UWTZ UCO
OWURF FBQT REW LAPASAUC SARQ UM
CQQOQO.   —NASS PUJYBC

88. BKXH APBBHM OMKLXT FHHM PLO
LWR DWYLPD FHDPSTH K DPL'R
TCHGG DWYLPD. —BKDXHV TCKGGPLH

89. YK AKSRTOW SK VE CYK SLT XYV
SBAOKAKO UVCY YRW ZLAKTCW, LTO
CYKT, XYKT YRW WKTCKTGK XLW
LUVBC CV UK ZAVTVBTGKO, ZHKLOKO
EVA SKAGD VT CYK QAVBTOW CYLC YK
XLW LT VAZYLT.   —LUALYLS HRTGVHT

90. GMA PAOG NATG GMLPZ GR NALPZ
VKAXAQ LT NALPZ CNKA GR HFRGA
TRJARPA YMR LT.

—JCQE IAGGLNRPA IRRKA

91. FRU REZYM ZQMV FHUYFG Y MUC
QVUY FRU CYA FRU XKVA FHUYFG Y
GFHYMSU JHKFUQM; QF HUPUWFG QF.

—J.X. ZUVYCYH

92. J IRDAZAUAJG RQWXZ ZR SK SROG
J CRQGHDAGW JGH OKEJAG J
SJUXKDRO.   —DJHT SAOH FRXGNRG

93. WKQQBE BE XBAK TONNSBQH DLN
TLQKS. XLCK POE QLWPBQH WL IL
ZBWP BW.   —FPSXXBE IBXXKN

94. BQTK LJD XGT UJBK XKU JDE
FJZTEQPKR XMBXLF EDGKF DI—XKU
PE PF DFDXMML EQT KJFTF JS LJDG
SGPTKUF.   —JGFJK BTMMTF

26

95. VL IA LVDXA OTK ETP'A XKMMQQE,
ADO, ADO INIVP. ARQP UKVA. PT
XQPXQ YQVPN I EIBP LTTH IYTKA VA.

—C.M. LVQHEX

96. H NJEPU BD ZFBCBTAFN ENEHIIU
SZRZHIN JKHJ JKZ OZNJ JATZ JB OEU
HCUJKACX AN IHNJ UZHS.

—THSJU HIIZC

97. NII JES EXX NRV KVIKXV LRI HGIL
RIL NI PTG NRV DITGNPM EPV JTFM
SPYQYGW NEBYDEJF EGS DTNNYGW
REYP.   —WVIPWV JTPGF

98. ONINKOLZ GNFFI WI GZKG
CBWOGNNR BWG BC KRM GNR
TRETHTEWKFI FTQN LZBLBFKGN.

—IKREOK VBMRGBR

99. RS'X DCS MQXZ PMRDJ Q ECSIML.
RK RS YMLM, KQSIMLX YCWFN NC RS.

—NCLCSIZ, "SIM JCFNMD JRLFX"

100. M BGMV EOWRRT MS VWP XMXVW
ZJKFP HPOKGEP RX ISPGCRSMK. SRV
HPOKGEP M WKF MV, HGV HPOKGEP M
ORGTFS'V EIPTT MV.   —JROYN ZJKDMKSR

101. WCJ'L HVVBQL FZWBO DFCY
OLFHJXB YBJ, HJW FBYBYGBF LUHL
HKK YBJ HFB OLFHJXB.   —FCGZJ YCFXHJ

102. N ABUK B QKBQAKOO
ZXOOKZJNXE; VBDTK DXR'UK QKKE
NJ? N GKKY NJ XE TKBZAKQ BOO
XUKC JAK LXCOS.   —QJKYAKE LCNHAJ

103. HJIO GZ EHP AIOOFRSHH QESQK
XAOP LE ASZ, "NJFP EXL YKSL ZEX
PEF'L PE YOHH, LKOF PEF'L PE JL."
                           —SHN, "SHN"

104. B'H OWEJUBXD OUBVR YL WYEG
YL B RKRE GBG. OWR TYII'L FALO XJO
DROOBXD OWRER YL QYLO.
                           —IRQOZ DJHRM

28

105. NBAX UG FZHARWGQLXG, LFFGMX
GLFI ZXIGQ KZQ OILX EZB LQG, LHW
WZH'X MZRHX ZBX XIG KLFX XILX XIG
ILRQ IG'A DZARHP ZH IRA IGLW RA
HZO PQZORHP ZBX ZK IRA HZAG—LHW
IRA GLQA.   —MGP UBHWE,
          "YLQQRGW ORXI FIRDWQGH"

106. C FIPX AXNNCHA GUCF—DOMN
NBX VUYN NBUN MIGXIHX FCYEXZ U
MNUGJ VIL SIO CM PXLS LXUMMOLCHA.
          —NBIGUM GUAHOG, GUAHOG J.C."

107. UT UTYT KAID SB RAWT USID DSF
...S ETRR AHI AE RAWT USID DSF, KHI
DT NSNB'I.   —MGL MGL CLKAY

108. N LBQ BE KFZKOOKEJ QJRSKEJ
REJNO JKE, BES JAKE VD VNES TKHBE
JX LBESKC.   —HCBZK YBOKD

109. DMCFFCU THC LXC VWPIQ, JWH
LXCV FXTMM AIXCHAL LXC ITLAWITM
UCDL.   —XCHDCHL XWWKCH

29

110. G EZCU BCU WC FC NZQWBGZO—
G'S N SCS.   —ACKJNZZJ INAA

111. LPDPJ SMMXE GXCJ TNVMQ BX
TSMM GXC RG GXCJ OVJAB LSIP. NP
NSAL'B ZLXEL GXC MXLU PLXCUN.

                         —OJSL MPRXEVBH

112. KYWSYBS AVA E KUQAN YD UIS
UITSS WYKU-YDUSB-ISETA LITEKSK VB
BSJ NYTG FVUN. YBS VK "ISN, UEPV."
UJY VK "JIEU UTEVB AY V UEGS UY
OZYYWVBCAEZS0'K?" EBA UITSS VK
"AYB'U JYTTN, VU'K YBZN E DZSKI
JYQBA."   —AERVA ZSUUSTWEB

113. OXP OXNPP-ZTNOFSF GKSDX FH
OXP PVFOEZP EW TZPNFDTS
PWWFDFPSDL. CXPNP PGHP DTS LEK
MPO TS PTNWKG, T APGGLWKG, TSJ T
HSEEOWKG TO OXP HTZP OFZP?

                         —MPNTGJ N. WENJ

114. NMPD OMTO KHDHT'V WJFH VM RXZH
NMP. VLJV'O KLJV UDJTFBLXRFDHT
JDH GMD.   —YJTH OWXRHN

115. KN HZYU SZXX VYLNTY FXX UIY
OFU OVNL QNRV DNHQ DYPFRMY UIY
DVFZK ZM YKUZVYXQ OFU. SZUINRU F
DVFZK QNR LZAIU XNNB ANNH, DRU
FXX QNR PNRXH HN ZM VRK ONV
WRDXZP NOOZPY.   —PNTYVU DFZXYQ

116. AMP ZFLGN TIVTZB MTXP AMP
BTHP ECFSIPH—MFV AF CPSPI TGQ
RFGOFCH TA AMP BTHP AKHP. AMPZ
MTXP BFIXPQ AMKB SZ QPOZKGN
AMPKC ETCPGAB TGQ RFEZKGN FGP
TGFAMPC.   —DLPGAKG RCKBE

117. UZ SCR ECNW AXW EVB VIG SCR
ECNW MCCG PVRPVMW, GCI'A BVAJX
WUAXWK CZ AXWH QWUIM HVGW.

                —QWAAS AVEHVGMW

118. OGLNJ JNRNC VIRN TGMJW LBJYU.

SVNT ICN HGCJ SVCNN SVGMUIJY TNICU

GKY.   —UVNKIWV YNKIJNT

119. VAZFDUDK FA BABGNUD ABPZPAZ,

FQM QGEFNM PE ZAF U ZMI SUZVM

EFMB—PF PE UZ ANS TGEPZMEE

BDAVMSGDM.   —RDUZ NMTAIPFL

120. E UESEBWNF NC E TEB DVW

ZBWDC E PNIIPY WO DVEI'C XWNBX

WB.   —DNPPNET LRSSWRXVC

121. NZ NJ MYRX'J ZSA IPNTS J.

ZYAXRMSAJP, NXGDXJSA SZ

JDTDGNRNSX, MD'C RJNTT ED DYJNXL

ZASUDX AYCNS CNXXDAR.

                        —FSPXXO KYARSX

122. EKM FUMTFQM, KMFHEKX, IMHH-

FNVYDEMN FNYHE QMED YJ FE

DMUMB-EKRTEX RB EKM CATBRBQ

LMMHRBQ VYDE JHFRB EMTTRPHM.

                        —VMFB GMTT

123. SOPEGS ZJUOH'P OUUG PJ
QJPEUB GU SHV GJBU CHMUOO T'G
SBJCHZ KTASBO JB ZJAO. PEU PETHA
PESP XJCMZ QJPEUB GU GJOP XJCMZ
QU S ZJA OGJFTHA S KTASB.

                         —OPURU SMMUH

124. T VRAQ WGNPX FVQ YQIF JRB FG
STAQ RXATEQ FG BGNL EVTHXLQP TI
FG WTPX GNF JVRF FVQB JRPF RPX
FVQP RXATIQ FVQZ FG XG TF.

                        —VRLLB I FLNZRP

125. J EJPOKS JE GMS RJTX CKS
CNJIS CG GMS SVT LE GMS TCZ, J'IS
TLVS UZ QLA.   —KLXSCVVS ACKK

126. CNTFT XFT EZFT MUTXHXYC
CNWYRH CZ PZ CNXY DTXC IM
MTZMUT.   —EINXEEP XUW

127. GSVOI GMM, LZGV XQ IOGMXVW
GCWLGW? CTVZXC' AKV G
NTMMONVXBO ZKCNZ. —DGCO LGJCOI

128. TNWD JDNJGD LKGG AKD ZWNT
CKR-NW-TKVV DPRKMX RCPM ZWNT
CKR-PMA-WOM AWKUKMX.

—AOMBPM CKMDV

129. HGX SOGE EIWK ZWSBJ KIQJ
AGXOKMH NMBWK? HGX VGO'K IWPB
KG FB EQKKH GM ATBPBM, WJ TGON
WJ HGX AWO IQMB JGZBGOB EIG QJ.

—KBV FWUKBM,
"KIB ZWMH KHTBM ZGGMB JIGE"

130. VJRENTV ND V KVEPR, QENRISKZ
SHP NI V AREZ DJVKK EHHJ. RAREZ
CNJR NC LVPD NCD CVNK, NC WIHTWD
HARE V TOVNE.   —VEIHKS CHZIURR

131. V KYD'O GIDO IDP "PTU-RTD"
IAYCDK RT. V GIDO TXTAPLYKP OY
OTNN RT OJT OACOJ TXTD VZ VO
WYUOU OJTR OJTVA EYLU.

—UIRCTN MYNKGPD

34

132. D NOVMOZX JPO RDOC IJOCDIB.
D NODGG CVQZ HJNO JA DO.

—HDWCVZG XVQDN

133. ZNBLEV RUA QCRK ZC ZNCVK FNC
FUBZ, IOZ CLXA ZNK ZNBLEV XKTZ IA
ZNCVK FNC NOVZXK. —UIDUNUR XBLQCXL

134. NHAHAOHN FCYFHN NTFHNQ KCK
HZHNGXRCYF SNHK MQXMCNH KCK,
ODX QRH KCK CX OMWJBMNKQ MYK CY
RCFR RHHEQ. —SMCXR BRCXXEHQHG

135. DZRU WBF JRMBOR PRUGQR, WBF
DBU'V YUBD GV. —JGQQ MBPJW

136. F DP QUI QW HVQGI TIQTZI AVQ
NCGH XDU'H VIZT MIHHFUM D OFXO
QCH QW ZFWI—IBIU AVIU FH'G D OFXO
FU HVI HIIHV. —TQZZK DLZIY

137. U JNMFOHUW TDQ OM U FUYCDQ
HUPO ZOHJ HJD ADHDY YSVVOVK.

—KYNSEJN AUYP

138. VSUOMGX KMBT GSBKFIC
SRSALBMZSJ MJ OMCS DSMGX GMDDOSV
BF VSUBT DW VLACJ. —SIMA JSZUISMV

139. ZJ UPQOHYZ HKYA KV
PYXQVXKHKVC ZJ CPQAA NSOKGA
EKGN ZJ VYG KVXQZY. —YPPQH BHJVV

140. FZLXR BWT WX SAKKXR KFJLZ,
OWX JAOASCAVZ FGXSCUFJ KFJL
SAKKXS BCMMCX ZVOOAJ CZ SXIVOXR
OA WFQX SXGFSLXR, "KXUFVZX
OWFO'Z BWXSX OWX GAJXT CZ."
                    —OWXARASX W. BWCOX

141. KD'E WJONTKPC DV CV VID YKDZ
SB JT-YKMJ RJFNIEJ EZJ NOWJNHB
APVYE K'S NP KHKVD.
                    —DZVSNE YNWWJP

142. NY'GY LHH QFGM QGLCY,
BGIOBPMD, LMA DGYYAJ, LMA EFOB FV
IO GYELPM DGYYAJ.
                    —EPDMFM EXHLIDRHPM

36

143. GR LNIOXVANRV JVSXNJ, JS
ADYP EGVYPNR NBDGIANRV GJ
MSDFPV GRLGJYXGAGROVNQT MT
INSIQN UPS CDJV YSAN GR HSX ANR'J
DRLNXUNOX.   —CDQGO YPGQL

144. RGQN KH RKLN ESN INVHRNH. ESN
GRZNO XGD TNE KE, ESN FGOHN ESN
VEEVBL.   —IVOX OGPNOEH OKUNSVOE

145. NAYX SLHER BQAE SGRLY HRW
WQR'X IAJO GRXQ XUL VAERGXAEL.
                    —YOLRMLE XEHMB

146. G OIDW FIGVWC IVC NMHX XOW
HIQW XWV SMRVCH HM QIVJ XGQWH
MDWP IVC MDWP IFIGV QJ YWNNRNGXW
QRHX OIDW CWLI DR.   —LIVW UIFVWP

147. U'BS QSSK IUPY RKO U'BS QSSK
JGGI. QSZUSBS LS, YGKSE, IUPY UX
QSHHSI.   —XGJYUS HAPVSI

148. DZNFN PFN HG PDZNJEDE GH
DWFQWXNHD PJFVXPHNE.—NFJRP KGHO
37

149. XSWA KFOFOHFK, GVLF TGS'KF

GQFK AYF YMUU TGS HFJMV AG NMLB

SN WNFFZ.   —LYCKUFW WLYSUD

150. IMFVF WVF IYTFB RJI IJ PCYVI.

NMFR DJQ'VF BYHA. NMFR DJQ'VF

NYIM HMYCOVFR. NMFR DJQ'VF JR IMF

NYIRFBB BIWRO.   —SJDHF SYCCBJR

151. HJIO WIO UITGJ EJIPU NPCEPIN

TOR UIEPUI, EJIQ DF EF APIGIN.HFWIO

DF UPDJE FO GFFLPOD.   —DTPV NJIIJQ

152. F SUHFZ SEU SWDD XLDD ELB FQL

SWDD XLDD FZKXEWZQ.   —BWXF HFL YBUSZ

153. EY EDA'Y AKJKDDRQZ YU MK QEJC

RAO HRVUXD YU MK CRTTZ. EY'D UAWZ

AKJKDDRQZ YU MK QEJC.   —RWRA RWOR

154. WPX QSO NLQPAL SNPXU SH

LYQCUCOR SH WPXZ TPPK NBLOKLZ.

UEL VCKH QPAL CO, BPPV WPX CO

UEL LWL, SOK SHV CT SOWNPKW'H

EPAL.   —LZAS NPANLQV

38

155. G'A KU KP KZH RYHP AL IKBE
ZVHM VCU AVWH UYKP G TV.

—QYLXXGM TGXXHW

156. L QSDDCAZ JLU BSRTZ MSDDSQ L
TSI SW IDSRMTA QCIN HDLBICBLTTG
US BSTTLIADLT.   —NATAU UCATVAU

157. J'A MDGFNJZI AV UJHD NF TDJZI
K XQVOBJKNYJO XKNJDZN. JN'Q K
GFOKNJFZ, UJRD TDJZI K ZEZ, FZUV K
UFN AFYD DWXDZQJGD.

—PFVOD YDTDNK-TEYMJNN

158. TLW QB G MYSLICGJR SY IQS
SLGU ALYAYEQSI? G BGRLS QU TIEE
DFUS QKKEW GS NGCIASEW SY BW
SLGRLU.   —CLYNQ BYCRIJUSICJ,
    "SLI BQCW SWEIC BYYCI ULYT"

159. BHWZ, K NHWP ZKTJRNB. VEJ KJ
PRHTO'J DWSH BRE OKAH. ZKJYHN
NHWP ZKTJRNB, JRR.   —XRWO NKIHNT

39

160. LHRHRUHL QOTQ TW T QHHFTBHL
GAS TLH TQ QOH JTWQ WQTBH KF
GASL JKMH VOHF GAS VKJJ UH OTYYG
QA OHTL QOTQ QOH YOAFH KW MAL
GAS.   —MLTF JHUAVKQN

161. MT SJKK FG KTAB LFMI RTWEYBKS
FY MIB SFEYM YBPEBM TS IJDDFGBYY.
MIBG FS RTW'EB GTM J NTTX QFVBE
RTW PJG JKLJRY SJKK ZJPC TG RTWE
TLG PTQDJGR.   —ETZBEM QTEKBR

162. Q RQCZ PMLZHXCXPFVD FV CFJZ
QL QNDX RZHYQLFH UYX YQV LZKZA
XULZG Q HQA.   —HQAAFZ VLXU

163. GINSXAGYU YM CMYTNS
NFDNSXNYAN WGAGEXMYU. EBNO
UXIDCO UMYO EBNI UM EBNO AGY
XTYMSN EBNI HMS EBN SNUE MH EBN
ONGS.   —LMBY TSXUBGI

164. LBH YBA'G MUIS GB VS YBJYL GB VS
U TMEQFGQUA.   —GUNNL XULS VUOOSE

40

165. RTVE BCR BWXTMK OIY TYPYKKOIE

BR UYYJ RTY'K CXQY WOJJE. RTY XK BR

VYB WYI BWXTU KWY XK WOGXTM WYI

RCT COE, OTL BWY RBWYI, BR VYB WYI

WOGY XB.   —VETLRT F. NRWTKRT

166. PXBM G PIV I YGJ RE TIOBMDV

RWKBJ ICWD—FND G ICPIEV LWNMJ

DXBR.   —OWJMBE JIMUBOLGBCJ

167. N AGNJI TJ-CAZPF JWLNAX NC

LNCPWCANJP, CGZRFBWD, ZJL LZRZPNJP

AT ZDD AGNJPC ZRFHNOZJ. UWA NB N KFHF

AKFJAX-AKT KNAG Z PHFZA UTLX, NA

KTWDL UF ZHANCANO, AZCAFBWD,

MZAHNTANO, ZJL Z MHTPHFCCNQF

HFDNPNTWC FVMFHNFJOF.

                 —CGFDDFX KNJAFHC

168. IVLVS WT AT B ZTGATS QXTDV

TUUKGV FEBIAD BSV ZVBZ.—VSCB HTCHVGJ

169. STHDO HRFOHZ, S PBAZ RSI S

LFUA BT FHI BGU.   —PDHHD LFAQDO

41

170. VRR RBVTK VSHYTI, WKLVTHP RB
DSRHPTKWKX VMT FWKP, FTSTIC
ITKXVMTKL VMT URKYTSLHVWRK.

                    —TIWGHDTVM PSTN

171. YHH PDAI OQNCAKJO—PDAU'NA
DECDSYU NKXXANO. SDU WK UKQ
PDEJG PDAU SAYN IYOGO SDAJ PDAU
SKNG KJ UKQ?   —YNZDEA XQJGAN,

                    "YHH EJ PDA BYIEHU"

172. FT EZC RMWWLC XLCTMT
KFCJFCQGL, Q WCMTW IZBT KZCL
WYFG IYLKQTWT.   —VZFG JMTTZB

173. SY OGV EVHENV RHF'O AQFO OH
DHBV HMO OH OGV EQIX, FHTHRK'U
PHFFQ UOHE OGVB.   —KHPS TVIIQ

174. VDX VQ SCX QPDDG SCHDZF
BLVPS SCX FSVMN YBUNXS HF SCBS
XKXUG SHYX VDX RXUFVD LPGF,
BDVSCXU FXWWF, BDA LVSC SCHDN
SCXG BUX BFSPSX.   —BDVDGYVPF

42

175. HUE GZHGUZ KXHFUEQ'I ZJI
XZJUIX RHHEK. IXZP QZZE JUU IXZ
GAZKZALJICLZK IXZP VJQ SZI.

— AHDZAI HADZQ

176. ZEK LNBK TNG BKMA MSNGZ
JNOQZQUX, ZEK LNBK TNG RNZ ZN
MALQZ ZEMZ KMUE JMBZT QX HNBXK
ZEMD ZEK NZEKB.   — HQOO BNRKBX

177. RG'H Z IZIV KVIHLM DSL DZMGH
GL SVZI DSZG SV WLVHM'G DZMG GL
SVZI.   — WRXP XZEVGG

178. Z VQBVER BVPFWX FH KWF ZPFH
GHQZFZTR, COF Z BVR PWIWM QZKUF
WPHOKU FH AVJW FUW FWVA.

— VMF COTUBVQX

179. QCHX RCOW NYDM RYV QCFX
JXCPK CP Y OXQXGWSPX JSSOW RCOW
YP SGXP ENJDXQQY—PS NYOOXD
RWCBW RYM MSE OEDPXZ, MSE KSO
CO CP OWX XMX.   — IXYP FXDD

43

180. LGJ MSN D AGFB XL UGMN GU
UMDR, XJV BAGSGFDIVI VUMWBR GS
DSOUMIVUJAVJUB. —FMUCMUBV VPMVAPBU

181. W NMT'Y QHSI RXHY WB RSWYYIT
HGMLY FI BM UMTO HB WY WBT'Y
YSLI.   —VHYXHSWTI XIZGLST

182. UQXUZQ RGX CHLGM CHTQ RHMG
CHTQ BJBOZZS QDY BU RHMG OJGQJ.
                    —OPHLOHZ AOD PBTQD

183. IUH RGQC HGB JMLQ TX YGDRC
UJGHQ, RQCFMBQ BNQ PUSB BNUB
CGIQBMIQC NQ NUC BG QUB BNQI.
                —URJUM Q. CBQLQHCGH

184. FPZOGACJI CU G MJIPFVHZW ASCIY.
CH BJZ OJZWPI'A UCYI BJZV IGEF, BJZ'P
SGTF AJ DGB OGUS. —VCAG EGF QVJMI

185. O EPOWN ML UOCEP TD EPR
DRTCSP LMC T YTCQRC TATCEZRWE.
                    —COET ZTR UCMHW

44

186. Z JZDS JCLF MOJDW,

SWYSXZOJJQ MTSL HTSQ OKS HODSL

UQ YSCYJS MTC OLLCQ RS.

—PKSA OJJSL

187. DWP KPRD PVPNGDJHP JR DWP

EUP AWE WQR RPURP PUEGBW DE YJNC

BEEI ZPU DE IE AWQD WP AQUDR IEUP,

QUI RPMX-FPRDFQJUD PUEGBW DE CPPY

XFEZ ZPIIMJUB AJDW DWPZ AWJMP DWPO

IE JD.   —DWPEIEFP FEERPHPMD

188. R GWKGUN FGJS G VTBOGORBA

DBM SJSMUOFRAE—RO NGJSN

BMRERAGW OFRAYRAE.

—ZBMBOFU W. NGUSMN

189. JIO JBMO HXVQ XOROB BOHJH;

JIOBO YH TASTPH T IYUIOB UVTA JV

TJJTYX, TXE JIOBO TBO, QP JIO HTGO

JVWOX, TASTPH GVBO TXE GVBO

NOVNAO JV AVVW EVSX MNVX.

—BMHHOAA APXOH

45

190. DN FAE RMB WY RMIA QMQDAZ,

WRAK TYJVB YEVK AIAG RMIA YEA

AMUR. —SGDEUAZZ BDMEM

191. TWX KMQ'D JFOJKD DW ARD DAJ

HMKGOWD RV TWX NWQ'D OXD M VJE

QRKGJBL RQ DAJ YMKARQJ.

—VBRO ERBLWQ

192. N XLBC QEQAHCVNMO NM CVQ

WLBC-MSCSX UQWAQBBNLM.

—QAYS TLYTQRJ

193. J ITBO 'AV IXA ICYIX MUO IXAH

LABB LTC JI. —ZYOEA XMCCH WITUA,

"UJEXI NTYCI"

194. DU DPEVKE VK KQXZOQSI FJQ

GPQSTHZK EJVUYK EJDE GZQGCZ

SQU'E UZZS EQ JDMZ.—DUSI FDPJQC

195. ZQLC HW HBDQLS QOM DB KLD

MVCCLS PBS LVKQD, TQL'M RETD HOYL

LCBEKQ PBS TVIDLLC OCM BCGW TLSUL

QOGP. —KSONVL OGGLC

46

196. EKC FZNA'C MHLYG ZG MEY

VYKDEM EKC UKGN CMKQQ PYWOCYC

MZ HIIYJM.　　　—MZGK IHNY FHUFHPH

197. L PBKKMNNZZ MJ L RGBDY NQLN

VZZYJ KMSDNZJ LSE TBJZJ QBDGJ.

　　　　　　　　　—KMTNBS WZGTZ

198. GPNDMDUQ DQ MTB CHM PY

NPPXDVW YPH MHPSRNB, YDVZDVW DM

BFBHEOTBHB, ZDCWVPQDVW DM

DVUPHHBUMNE, CVZ CGGNEDVW MTB

OHPVW HBJBZDBQ.　　　—WHPSUTP JCHI

199. TK UR KTW LY PBR KRURS, PLJR

TYM PLMR UTLP XQS YQ JTY.

　—RM YQSPQY, "PBR BQYRWJQQYRSK"

200. GAPZHP EBKPNHIZBK ILP NPZHSB

MLQ WLYBPHP JPOPIZUAPH IZHIP HS

OSSK. YI YH HYFGAP. ILP WLYBPHP

KS BSI WSSX ILPF, ILPQ VEHI

ILNPZIPB ILPF!　　　　—VPRR HFYIL

47

201. WXOQO NH G KNRO UNRO FOWZOOR

KNHXNRE GRP HWGRPNRE SR WXO

FGRV UNVO GR NPNSW. —GRSRATSYH

202. COU GYYUHQY ZU LM GNNULGQCUYB.

COU JREMRVCGCJCGMRQY CQDUV Q

YGCCYU YMRHUX. —OURXB Q. DGVVGRHUX

203. Q KAYQL DL HAIZ KDHH TA QHYAEO

QLGOVDLF JAC Q YQL, ZMUZWO FDIZ PW

OVZ TZEDCZ OA DYWCAIZ VDY.

                    —LQOVQLDZH SCQLTZL

204. HD VJLYL QKW KAT ZGWVHXL HA

VJHW QPYNI, PHN XPFSKAT LULXGVHCL

OKVJYPPFW QPGNI WFLNN NHEL VJL

PALW HA VJLHY RKW WVKVHPAW

                    —ZPJAAT XKYWPA

205. NK IFU'E FBB XK YKGVKR

XKIFSRK RVCKXVOD YFR EV RLE VU

EYK ISGX FUO IBFM FR EYKD PV XD.

                    —NLBB GVPKGR

48

206. TFIIBY JMY FQ XVYW PKN'OY SJEYI
XFUV UXK UYTRUJUFKWQ JWI PKN EVKKQY
UVY KWY UVJU XFBB MYU PKN VKTY GP
WFWY K'EBKEZ.   —OKWJBI OYJMJW

207. AC A VJF YUPTU A TJW NPAUN
XP SALM XVAW SPUN, A'F VJLM XJYMU
HMXXMZ RJZM PC OGWMSC.
                        —MDHAM HSJYM

208. UDI YLR CU FIC AMFA NQUUK
OXIBBZXI MB CU FU TUZDCLMD
PQMTNMDF USIX TUQIAMQQB.
                        —ILXQ YMQBUD

209. RVIR OFBEY ZJ I WFFY RVKLW
XFA RVJS RF HBR FL SP RFSZNRFLJ:
OVJAJQJA NVJ OJLR, KLHEBYKLW
VJAJ, KR OIN IWIKLNR VJA ZJRRJA
UBYWSJLR.   —YFAFRVP MIATJA

210. HL CMY AGC MGT XHCCYOT HO
CMY WDYO, CMGC BWO'C JGXY 'YJ
ZHTAEHCT.   —YUHTGZYCM WVHUDHY

49

211. FJRYQMRR YR B NHHC NBUM—

SHXR HZ GHUWMXYXYHQ BQC B

UYQYUJU HZ AJSMR. THJ IMMW RGHAM

EYXO UHQMT.   —QHSBQ FJROQMSS

212. NIBUJE I ZIZR UT FUAP WIAUJE

RMOG FMVPG FUQ IJK LMGHUJE UW

MBPG RMOG NPIK.   —HIGMF ZOGJPWW

213. AFRQC KWKHVIS RM RJKWSXIQX.

WXOFSPRMF KFWKVF JRCOX QWX

VRGF BWH.   —JRJR KWQN

214. NRYJSCJAJ RW VCUN BMRHJ

JDJAQ VJW NJLRWIN, VCJAJ UN F

SRYFW BUDUWB HUAVC VR F LCUMI.

NCJ YKNV HJ XRKWI FWI NVROOJI.

                        —NFY MJDJWNRW

215. HRYFY'G HRFYY ACAYBHG WB V

AVB'G OWSY: KRYB RY UIMG V RCIGY,

V ZVF, VBT V BYK ZCOCF HJ. HRVH'G

KRVH VAYFWZV WG VOO VUCIH.

  —VFZRWY UIBPYF, "VOO WB HRY SVAWOM"

50

216. GNNXRTFF PO HNX T QNHXTQX
OJNWX. PX'O T QNFFPOPNH OJNWX.
VTHQPHY PO T YNNV DKTIJFD NG T
QNHXTQX OJNWX. —VLGGM VTLYZDWXM

217. AL EUKW UG O CUBNF WOFWP...OG
GIIT OG UF'G CUBNF, GNW GFOPFG FI
WOF.   —NWTTL LIYTBAOT

218. COK PLJYDILCN WKCTKKF D
IKJCDVIDFC'J YILUK DFP XGGP
HVDSLCN ILJKJ LF PLIKUC
YIGYGICLGF CG COK JLQK GX COK
YKYYKI ZLSS.   —WINDF ZLSSKI

219. KSX YCSO, ZV KSX IQSSL PT,
KSX'MM MSIT N MSL SV LQTIT
QXPNCZLNBZNC NONBWI.
            —FQTAK FQNIT, "VMTLFQ"

220. DBYH CT X CXM HBY KYTDM'V
CXUT CPDVXUTD XMK P'EE DBYH SYF
X CXM HBY KYTDM'V KY XMSVBPMN.
            —VBTYKYZT ZYYDTOTEV

51

221. T'LV QVLVWAGVQ R PVH
GYTWANAGYI—T APWI QFVRQ APV QRI
RM R MTOV.   —ZYRFWVN NZYDWJ

222. PJ RKZV MIN K SGKVN SRA AG
SXGVV SKPVB KI SXV QMBS ZAGSJ
JVMGB SA XMLV WGVMTZMBS SAYVSXVG,
WFS KS RMB BA NKBMYGVVMWQV RV
XMN SA BSAU. —RKIBSAI OXFGOXKQQ

223. R CHUO PNHJOZ JC LO NH
NJAORXJ, LFJ R BNYO FE—JAOI ANYO
HC ACKRZNIX.   —AOHHI ICFHBSNH

224. MAA N IPIX JIIFIF QZ RJZS N
AIMXJIF NJ RNJFIXOMXQIJ. FZJ'Q UNQ
VIZVAI. EAIMJ CV WZCX ZSJ BITT.
                    —XZGIXQ DCAOUCB

225. CBTECZVY SXLVBEYP CEY
STPULBYEYB IT ZY IXY MYPYECV
QETQYEIO TA IXY XRDCP ECSY. ERBY
SXLVBEYP ZYVTPM IT IXYLE DTIXYEU.
                    —WRBLIX DCEILP

52

226. JQ'X FEQ QAWB J UGH FEQUJFK
EF. J UGH QUB AGHJE EF.

—OGAJTMF OEFAEB

227. KSV IVHZFKM CU EQXXVEE RE KC
YV YCJVW YM IVCIFV OSC QEVW KC
EHQY MCQ.   —HZHXM ZEKCJ

228. M OIEJ I YPAGJCTBK NILJ-BF
RCJY. ZOJV'CJ ZOJ XINJ FJPFKJ
CJXZPCMAQ ZOJ XZIZBJ PT KMHJCZV.

—HPH OPFJ

229. ZDFM PDFB WSOO PDF GXOO UM
PDF IFMSPF, PDF IFMSPXGI YX MXP
QMXZ ZDFPDFG PX SMIZFG "NGFIFMP"
XG "MXP KJUOPB."

—PDFXYXGF GXXIFTFOP

230. LXBVXYYXB TZ X BXEEWS
TZMXBK WAA YVU DWXZY WA BUS
FUEZUP KUCWYUK YW YVU JNEZNTY
WA MNBDV.   —EXPLWBK ZWOWMWC

231. GQBOG LEBQ PBODTVX, TXEQH
LEBQ PBODTVX, TVX UHG TO KBJP TO
LEB JTV AV LEBQ EIV VTKH.

—METV QANHQO

232. A HOIOC OZE AH Z COJEZSCZHE
EXZE'J BIOC Z XSHVCOV MOOE BMM
EXO QCBSHV ZHV LBH'E JEZHV JEAWW

—UZWIAH ECAWWAH

233. YCHNB CES WBA LZPYS YCHNBG
LTWB KZH, GEZPA CES KZH GYAAV
CYZEA.   —JPG. VCWPTRD RCJVMAYY

234. UBA ABS'J ZRPN SB ZMOJRPNO—
JERJ'O EBF EN UBJ JB LN UBA.

—RTGEMN LXSPNT,

"RDD MS JEN QRZMDH"

235. M YMVLW EZW UEZX LZX WZ PNQ
WLMIWG-AZPI XZITN XLQIQ WLIQQ
XZPRT TZ, KPW WLDW TZQN EZW YQDE
M TZE'W UEZX XLDW M'Y WDRUMEV
DKZPW.   —IPWL NLDGN

236. Y XDRJ GXJK PI VBBR VDTTL
DLTJJW FEZYKU RXJ FDI SJODELJ Y
CKBG YR'L UBYKU RB SJ EW DTT
KYUXR.   —LRJWXJK GZYUXR

237. AED JLDRR NPVC PAJRD NRPJL,
LPSD PFN ASFORDFPSIC UEFJSFZR JE
ODEG, TZJ MLEFR UPIIC JPMRD EAA.
                          —XELFFV UPDCEF

238. G ONYNB UTOGQ SFNO G ANJ
HDWJ. G KCWJ QFTOAN SFNBN G STOJ
JD AD.   —BGJT BCPONB

239. RSD URS VZL MLKF XL R
TFDJZNRXBNFX LCMZX XL ZRWK ZNF
ZKRH KERUNSKH. —FRUCKA MLAHVDS

240. R SVYU JVO WV KPFFUM HLPF
JVO AV, NOF AV JVO LPYU FV AV DV
KOXL VC RF? —ZUPW RSSDSUJ-XSPMTU

241. YZ'X H XLHSS FTESA, PWZ Y
FTWSAD'Z FHDZ ZT UHYDZ YZ.
                          —XZVUBVD FEYJBZ

242. CFYG KDRKND IJR PCFAPYD ZJDG
FWD NPQD IPWDB FWD RYNG BJRSVPYA.

—CFWG KDZZPORYD KRRND

243. G JWLGH FWYM HWB ZKYGE QHBW
CWVK DWVMY GHF RUYGH QB PWK PVH.

—KQRE MQLWH, "MQLWH GHF MQLWH"

244. LURNSQ LZNANR YNH YZSQ OYZ
OKU IUHO QZIZNRXRA MUJH XR OYZ
DUWROLG—TLZHXQZRO UC OYZ
WRXOZQ HONOZH NRQ LNQXU
JLUNQDNHOZL UC OYZ DYXDNAU
DWJH.   —AZULAZ KXSS

245. CD'L EQXRBHUWI DQ VB PJHHCBR
DQ JX JHNSJBQIQACLD—DSB QIRBH
KQW ABD, DSB PQHB CXDBHBLDBR SB
CL CX KQW.   —JAJDSJ NSHCLDCB

246. PFBRAYRS YR FCM QYAAWM EX
FCM UEBA YP LMUJ ABRSMUEIP; JEI SMF
VRENVMA AETR DJ FCM FUBXXYN XUEQ
DEFC PYAMP. —QBUSBUMF FCBFNCMU

56

247. B HG HZAV JBSI KXWII HOC BO

KXI OIBYXLVWXVVC VJ VOI KXBWKE.

BK BA H OIBYXLVWXVVC B QVTZC

ZBMI KV YIK VTK VJ.

—JZHOOIWE V'FVOOVW

248. BW'Y UMW WCXI WNFW ABLI BY

MUI PFOU WNBUZ FLWIC FUMWNIC—

BW'Y MUI PFOU WNBUZ MKIC FUP

MKIC.   —IPUF YW. KBUDIUW OBAAFR

249. H'OP FRZ JKFP FHWG PBVHZM JQ

UBQ BSFKWW VIP SKRZVFQ VIBZ HZ

BTT JQ CFHOHZM.   —CRZSBZ IHZPW

250. W'Y LZGI VKH-PDBMWVEZH. W

JZKWZLZ SMDS TZVTKZ BMVQKH BSDI

YDGGWZH PVG KWPZ, KWRZ TWAZVEB

DEH XDSMVKWXB.   —FVVHI DKKZE

251. CJBSWM QAAW TWLFLTRJO SW

CSMC YZCFFR SY WFH DTYH ZJTYA

EFO QFFI LTQRSZJHSFW.

—EOJW RAQFGSHP

57

252. GKSPS UPS DUP GAA NUTZ NST
WT MACWGWFE UTR TAG STAIHK
SCESBKSPS.   —KSPNWATS HWTHACR

253. TD YQXJU, UQN ANYU UQTDB UX
LX TY ANQVEN TD V ZVDDNJ
ANSTUUTDB XDN'Y VBN. TS KXM VJN
YTRUNND XJ MDLNJ, UJK DXU UX BX
AVCL.   —PXXLK VCCND

254. YA'I HKA AUO LOH YH LF ZYTO
AURA QKBHAI, YA'I AUO ZYTO YH LF
LOH.   —LRO DOIA

255. IJ BKWIVBEU BE TJW NYT, TJ
JTUBHBJZ UYIU I STEW EQWVVE
RWUUWS UYIJ I HIRRIZW, HTJHVCKWE
UYIU BU NBVV IVET QIGW RWUUWS
ETCA.   —Y.V. QWJHGWJ

256. V NDRORD EPR KPVARTR
QREPMW MO RUEVAL...CMG KUA WM
UACEPVAL UE EPR EUZFR RJKRNE
UDQ HDRTEFR.   —XROO TQVEP

58

257. V XSKJ S LVARQJ RXVQNLNRXB.
DVQQ MXSC'L JARCB. JARCB MXSC'L
DOQQ. LTFSCTX MXJFJ VC VCTXJL.

    —SQVTJ FNNLJKJQC QNWHMNFCX

258. BDGA UEKAO MBB ESAH MKAHDIM,
KZ KEFNAH IEOQHEOFAP FHMJAPZ MOP
PAMFN UDFN IEBP NMK MOP LABB-E CMBMP.

  —GASDO MHOEBP, "FNA UEOPAH ZAMHC"

259. QKBIBLBT RUGBUIB XRHR GB YA
Y QXIO QXOBT QYOK GN RDUODK, Y RXN
Y'G OKYTRON, IUO SYTON. —WUB B. CBQYR

260. DBGQ PJN YSRG IYJQG, PJN KIQ
HG UNAG FBIF FBG VGAUJQ DBJ
UMNGGLGZ FBG FJJFBVIUFG FNHG SQ
FBG WSZZYG DIUQ'F KJWWSFFSQE I
BJUFSYG IKF.   —GYYGQ EJJZWIQ

261. PJ UWT LXYEV JB BRREH JB FX
JUWJ APZX PT W TJWYX P'F YBPVY
JUHBEYU.   —XAAXV YBBCFWV

262. TAFJY-YZJH WHGZTSW ST GFY YAZ

EFJTY WKKOSPYSFG SK MFL AWQZ WG

SJSTA KOWSJ KFJ YAZ TWLPZ

—GFJHWG HWSOZJ

263. SFIP MFFZ PXFWF YES'P RF ESK

YWOUOU. HK UYXFQCNF OU ENWFEQK

GCNN.   —XFSWK E. ZOUUOSDFW

264. UMA HVWDJLMI FQ QV

APUJDVJRFWDJFYI TQASTY. OMAW

GJFUDFW OFWQ D GDUUYA, QMA QMVTUQ,

"ZVR QDEA UMA NTAAW"; OMAW QMA

YVQAQ, QMA EVUAQ RVOW UMA KJFHA

HFWFQUAJ.   —OFWQUVW LMTJLMFYY

265. INR'Z PNJJS XENTZ XFNGIGRB

ZWUYZXZGNR. XC SNT BJNP NDIWJ,

GZ PGDD XFNGI SNT.   —QNWS XIXUC

266. ZIMB EIAO CFOY SFOJ'PO

ELTTOZ; ELSB SLXO AOBBLMOB LYZ

MOS VLEX SI JIQ.   —ALPJ VTJ

267. H LYHKR RSKVSFAAO YSND S VAAJ
JDSC. H CHRD LYSL XATZY ODLTX. H'J
YSND S ESEB HW HL MATCJ GSLTFD
HK S YSKJESV.   —FHLS FTJKDF

268. FQYFQFRH, FR DIJVZ CK RFTK IQ
EQ KPI RBFS YIB EVV F NQIG.

                     —WEQK GEPQKB

269. DWNR T PTR ESKE DSKW T
XVNKKM FSVO YGV TR WGIV, SK ENNPE
OSUN T PSRIKN. LIK ONK WSP ESK GR
T WGK EKGAN YGV T PSRIKN—TRH SK'E
OGRFNV KWTR TRM WGIV. KWTK'E
VNOTKSASKM.   —TOLNVK NSREKNSR

270. RGD VZR HM ODQEDBS
BNMCHSHNM DWBDOS ENQ NMD SGHMF
—RGD VZR CDZC.

                     —PTHMBX, "PTHMBX"

271. JFEBIFXXI EY QFMQ UXLIHPGVB
QEAH UFHL MBB ZXV LHHI QX IX QX
BXYH UHENFQ EY KMQFH.   —MLXLZAXVY

61

272. SQFARDK QDG R CQTJ QD

MDGJFWBQDGRDZ. R'A QOOHEJG BH

GQBJ HBCJF AJD, QDG CJ'W QOOHEJG

BH GQBJ MZOI EHAJD.

—OQTJFDJ, "OQTJFDJ QDG WCRFOJI"

273. GPHUSOYQ TPEGV RP YV GSO EV

VPGVYLIP EV Y ET, EGW DVFQRSOYQ

TPEGV OREO RP YV PJPG NSUVP OREG

TF LUSORPU-YG-IEN.—MEUI TPGGYGXPU

274. MG MU DNMWZ GVBMKO GJ OZG

ZEZVBGNMKO UGVTMONG MK LB NZTQ

GNTG M OZG RJKPFUZQ.

—LTVB EMVOMKMT LMRXT

275. SCLIL'U OR UBVC SCEON MU M

UBIL SCEON. SCMS'U HCT SCLT VMKK

ES NMFDKEON. —RUVMI FMXEURO,

"SCL RXX VRBAKL"

276. "TOKSYXSOSGX-HPXX" RVROWWM

TXOSV YQOY ZQXS KY CPXONV, KY

GOS'Y CX HKEXA. —OSLSMTLRV

62

277. QVJIGHJ KWG WQU QVJ HGEIL GT
LWC RVMCVERLJ GN LWC
NCUGENBCTESVCUU GT Q XSEDICN
VCZCN MGL Q IRSS TNGD GVC.

       —MCGNMC DCQVJ

278. FWPL OWWC A TSNW LG LSCW EQ
YGDDWXW SHLALMVW LWKL. AF EQ
TAXT KYTGGD, LTWQ VAVF'L WNWF
LWSYT SHLALMVW.

       —LGFQ ZSFLS, "LSPA"

279. NFTH KZFKPZ LF WFH QFWTMLZG
LXJW HF EZ XW XHHGXQHMSZ
ZAKZGMZWQZ—RWPZTT HYZI XGZ
THMPP RK.   —ZPPZW VFFLNXW

280. X LOC DOXIE XWM PB CXE
UMTEPROIOR UVPU BM EOIGO KOOL
COQQPTWBMT; LMIBSTXBOQD, QPFO
TXAMQOMT, PB NOB PBE CXBOIQMM.

       —IOTO GOXSH

63

281. ZIDWD INV NHXNSV MDDU N PQQJ

EWQTDVVQW RU ZID LRZTIDU. MGZ

QUTD GEQU N ZROD VID XNV

GVGNHHS TNHHDJ ZID ORVVGV, QW

OQO.　　　　　　　—VGD MDWLONU

282. T SG BSPEUB MTFU S GJONCTPJ

TH S HCZTOP KSGD; T FHJX XESP T

JCAEP PJ ZJ, QCP T ZJH'P FHJX

XEUBU PJ QUATH.　—OPUDEUH QSVHU

283. Q FGQMZ AO UTMXQEOV FTT

RCUG FGO ITTE WCUZ TY FGO OKVWP

LQVE, KME MTF OMTCIG TY FGO LKE

WCUZ TY FGO OKVWP ATVR.

　　　　　—YVKMZWQM E. VTTXOJOWF

284. WY NQM ZCFCD BRZG GQ XCC R

LRZ RARWZ, XRN, "W EQFC NQM. W

BRZG GQ LRDDN NQM. W BRZG GQ

PRFC NQMD HPWESDCZ." GPCN ECRFC

XOWS LRDOX.　　　—DWGR DMSZCD

64

285. PYW SLJ XFLU L ZFIINJV EY
GLEFI, QWE PYW ZLRF EY GLXB
IFLXXP TLOE YI EZFP UNF.

—IYOF JPXWJU, "EZF VYXUFJ VNIXO"

286. LT YSLQLPRZA ERPOWU OG BSLPU
NFAOLYW OG R XRZO, OXWM YGFZU UG
LO CM CRPULPB OGBWOXWS RPU RZZ
VZWRULPB PGO BFLZOM.

—UGSGOXM ESLBXO ELZAGP

287. P KRGO UG L NPRO, WKUSR UMM
NSPGVPGE LGN ZRLDC RLOPGE, LGN
PG MUXSORRG NLCW P ZLN TUWO
RFLIOTC OKU KRRVW.   —YUR R. TRKPW

288. YGHB SMZWCA. HCXHBY HTYXAI
GSA JSNTA—TN ZHGGAI XSN ACYA OY
OT GSA PHI.   —QHPL CAZZNT

289. EZ OZKHBTJUJZU EUUHAZJQ KEZ
XJREQ E UAOER IHA QJEAC HA BHZUDC.
E KHBTJUJZU EUUHAZJQ KEZ XJREQ
HZJ JPJZ RHZFJA.   —JPJRRJ Y. QHNZFJA

65

290. LGT LGNHX N THZADTK QAJL
RTOT ENJNLJ WOAQ VGNPKOTH. LGTD
KNK HAL RCHL SBUPNV AWWNVT.

                —GTOUTOL GAAETO

291. FI FGBRUD XYKXIQ PQUJ BG QXI:
"BRU GYJUD IGP LUB, BRU EUBBUD
IGP LUB-PAYUQQ IGP'DU X EXAXAX."

  —DGQU AIYPAJ, "BRU LGYJUA LWDYQ"

292. M QRGMRYR ISPI ML RYRZ M SPT
IX EZPNIMNR NPFFMQPGMWB, M BMCSI
BPFPCR ML ISRZR VRZR RFXJCS
IPZZPCXF PZXJFT.   —OPBRW QRPZT

293. Y'Z JYNV PT AV JCGNF VWTCHL
KT PLBP Y GTCJZ PLSTD PLV KTBI
BDBF BMPVS PLV JVPPVSK BSV DTSW
TMM.   —BWZF STTWVF

294. KJLB LHLDSRBL XT RIW WR ALW
SRI, CFDFBRXF XT RBYS ARRZ
WJXBMXBA.   —ERJBBS QLHLD,

        "KMDC, OXBOXBBFWX"

295. BM NMPSZM IKSDMFPMJGF BAMJ
GAM BSUKF GAIG IKXDGF MVPAIJRM
BLGA SJM IJSGAMU NMPSZM
LJGMDDLRLNDM GS XF. —JIGIDLI RLJCNMUR

296. WZQHCIKDLP VE Z OANZO
KCJLAABVQN VQ XUVLU PJI KID PJIC
YJQAP VQ PJIC KZQDE KJLHAD ZQB
NVSA PJIC LJZD DJ PJIC LCABVDJCE.

　　　　　　　　　　　　　—MJAP ZBZYE

297. UTBQWLXRIARGMB? ML'W B
JXHBJNQT NHBX RN WBDLB UTBQW.

　　　　　　　　—KMDDMH GBXGBXMDR,
　　　　　　　　"YHTURFH GBUC, CRLLHX"

298. XQB XV RCB HPXSZBU XV QBF
EXSJ ZU ZRU BRCQZM VXXO, WQO
XQPE IMOXQWPO'U WQO NLSHBS JZQH
BGLWPZYB LU WPP. 　　—TXCQ MXSSE

299. HACQ UNE XAHHXQ HM LM IAHU
ARGARAHP MV YQXXP LMWJURWHE.

　　—HUMCNE CNJRWC, "CNJRWC, B.A."

67

300. EC XQXAFJOX EV MIEOBEOH DYEBX,
MIXO VJTXWJRF EVO'M MIEOBEOH.

       —HXOXADY HXJAHX KDMMJO

301. K'B FPKJF AP BU ZVUDCPWJWOUVA
PJR BPTR URWT, ACRJ K'B FPKJF AP
OPMTERV.   —LPPEU WOORJ

302. HQQI JMFFIYVH GQVPYPCP YV
GQVGFBWYVH ZQE TOGZ EF CZYVR QU
QOMPFWXFP BVI ZQE WYCCWF EF CZYVR
QU CZF QCZFM DFMPQV. —TBMR CEBYV

303. SQO SWHIZGO YPSQ SQO WCS
WCLO PN SQCS OKOM PE RHI YPM,
RHI'WO NSPGG C WCS. —GPGR SHTGPM

304. N GNKH TL RQKOTRV JQXH KONR
N CXHRZO JHNK IQNC KONK'L ONM N
ZQBGIH ZQZPKNTIL.   —ZNXQI ZBKIHX

305. PCJLCPUS PJ TYPCI UAV JLBV
UAPCI YWVK LCT YWVK LILPC, QOU
VFXVGUPCI TPZZVKVCU KVJOHUJ.

          —KPUL BLV QKYRC

306. DZG MSEKD EHT MQB LEOSH'J
FSEKHST EHMJLZHV—ZJ'D NLZJS NZHS
NZJL LSKDLSM WEKD.

—LEKOSM WEKKQD, "REYZHV JLS VKETS."

307. AR NW PRRI FT ERNXW, NMA AR
AWBOZ RAZWJT AR NW PRRI FT WGWE
ERNXWJ—BEI XWTT AJRMNXW.

—VBJD AQBFE

308. CR ASDJWJKJVW VD H
QSAIWAHWOR JF HW HJQNHZ JW H
TVUJKJOJHW'F OHQ. —UHQQR YHZCHW

309. QFRTH MPR'E SIH JPDDVRTLL,
SIE VE NVWW ATE HFI P STEETG
MWPLL FB QTQFGVTL.—GFRPWZ GTPAPR

310. KLAQKFIAKI: NA FAAIW YLFKI
VGNV SNWAQ RQ VGNV QLBIMLJZ FQ
CLLDFAO.   —G.C. BIAKDIA

311. PTG PNJOL BTN AJSBL FS BTFL
TGELN? F QG, JSQ F JKLG PJLT JSQ
FOGS BTNV.   —QNSSFL BTJBHTNO

69

312. LUII PY DV LUBNJPQR YRUYNM
PM INY UMXRIRY, SUQWGPMX QGR
FPJKY WGUMXR WNINJY UMK LUII
LJND QGR QJRRY. —KUBPK IRQQRJDUM

313. M NZA EQ YZBL ENL YZBEC, M
TZC WLZI-CNZWLA. M TZC Z GME
ALWILCCLA GLBZDCL M NZEL WLZIC.
—BNZIXQEEL GMJVNZO

314. YDGC XQHGY TDIHR DSHV PWJC
NCCS TWYK QS DSC AWV: YTECCS
KCYKY ACEC LQJCS WSR KPC HDYCEY
LDK KPC OWEKY. —LCSC YPWHQK

315. NGH SBG EBL LN SBQ BU SH UABU
AH HGQHQ ATL VHUUHX: MHEBXH. ONZ
ETVV GHKHX CHU NZU NY UATL ENXVQ
BVTKH. —RNAG LUHTGMHIP

316. HKBPDLBPH U VPYHKJ SUH DK QK
U MPYW ZKJQ OLHDUJFP KCD KX SLH
GUW DK FKBP RUFA U HSKYD OLHDUJFP
FKYYPFDZW. —POGUYO UZRPP

70

317. DSH LSCCE JTSG CZO KHXOI
MONSKO DSH AET MKOEJ 'OQ.
SCZOKGVIO, VC'I BHIC TS NHT.

 —ISTTD AKSAJOCC, "QVEQV PVAO"

318. NQO UTSSOIOYPO FONEOOY ATSO
RYU NQO JLCTOD TD NQRN R DPITKN
QRD NL JRBO DOYDO RYU ATSO
ULODY'N. —XLDOKQ A. JRYBTOETPH

319. QT DTUWMMWYUVQM DB BICWITW
ZXI YQT MDBUWT UI UXW ZDMMDQC
UWMM IFWHUVHW QTL TIU UXDTG IP
UXW MITW HQTKWH. —QTITJCIVB

320. FZA WRXF HPXFAUEV "QYPSC
MYPSC" SC PWAYSTP FRMPK SX FZA
MYPSC SC FZA LSFTZAC XSCL.

 —AVSIPQAFZ DREVM MPOSX

321. "VRWYP" HKLVJ EG BVAELVB PG
WXPW UXETX JKQ XPDV EL JKQY
ZKGGVGGEKL OQGW SVAKYV WXV TPY
SYVPFG BKUL. —PLKLJHKQG

71

322. JYHYDHRK RJ LPXDX FPX

ZXCXGQEXD HYGGZQUXJ QYF FPX

FDXXJ, FPXA AKVXJ FPX JFDXXFJ

KWFXD FPXV.   —HRGG CKYBPA

323. ZHXZUH IX CWDFB CWEC DQ

CWHT EPXDI CWH CMVCW, DC GDKWC

YWEFKH CX OXGHCWDFK NHCCHM

NHQXMH CWHT WEPH CX WHEM DC.

                    —GEMOWE FXMGEF

324. B XZWWHKHWN HW WLKZLFZ RAL

SBF OLLM BN NAZ OBFT LV KHOM BFT

ALFZC BFT WZZ LFOC SBOLGHZW BFT

SALOZWNZGLO.   —BFLFCKLDW

325. BS PXH XYURQ DMCL

KHWMIQBGHC RIMQL RQC

SKYOPKRPBMQ, AHMAEH VMYEC

QHZHK KYQ URKRPXMQO, XRZH

DRDBHO, MK AERL DROHDREE.

                    —WRKEPMQ SBOT

72

326. S'D DLJ FXLF DAYUE GATYFK

CAW UBUWEFXSYR SY FXSK PAWZJ—

LYJ FXLF S JAY'F XLBU LYE.

                —LZUM WUSRUW, "FLMS"

327. WFOFPCXCZU CX JU CUPFUWCZU

WNJW YFLHCWX EZS WZ TF

FUWFLWJCUFG CU EZSL OCPCUR LZZH

TE YFZYOF EZS KZSOGU'W NJPF CU

EZSL NZHF.   —GJPCG MLZXW

328. DMGY DL GBL SX INB AGBLHYX'

QMSZRBLH; DMGY DL OLQIVL SX INB

QMSZRBLH'X AGBLHYX.

                —VLBBSY VGZZIE

329. KNI SCMI KNCSQ FVPEK VICSQ F

MIYIVLCKU CD KNFK ZNIS UPE VPLI

WIPWYI, KNIU KNCSR CK'D KNICL

AFEYK.   —NISLU F. RCDDCSQIL

330. DJQSU UZM UBEM LM PDT EDWM

UZM MTAK EMMU, KQEMJQAC EQOMK

UZM MTAK.   —ZMVJMVU ZQQOMV

73

331. X'Z NMW HCDKXKCNW TMI UIVAIN
NI NCGW IUU MWV MCN JWUIVW OMW
NMVWT XN XD NMW VXDA.

               —AVCHXW CFFWD

332. QIYVL YXQ VYTIC YXQ
KLWQEWJVL! VLIJI'C XIZIJ YXS
KFXZIXWIXV VWOI HFJ YXS FH VLIO!

               —OYJUYJIV OWVKLIGG

333. I XIEIHBM BC YEP KTY MIE'H
MTIEFP TBC NBEZ IEZ KYE'H MTIEFP
HTP CQRLPMH. —KBECHYE MTQVMTBWW

334. D KHI'Y TEIY YH EFPDXRX
DWWHCYENDYM YPCHAJP WM THCG, D
TEIY YH EFPDXRX DWWHCYENDYM OM
IHY KMDIJ.   —THHKM ENNXI

335. QELA ZUHA TUFAO RLBAQZN,
IBQYULQ PMDDAEO UE JZMOYBDW
ZBWYQO. BJ NUL YAME PAZZO, WAQ
NULE AMEO TYATSAV. —AEBTY OAWMZ

         74

336. QMDN MG AMJKS OVR WVND HN
JHSR AXZN HSE JHBKVT DYXSZN HN X
EM. DYKR WVND EMS'D AKHF DYKJ HQQ
HD DYK NHJK DXJK. —EMQQR THFDMS

337. RJN XSXARDYW MDPRB PNVDYKI
D LYRDW FDIJYKZRSK YKIRYRERYSK,
RJN SUUYXYDW YKRNWWYZNKXN
IBIRNV.   —TDPTDPD JSFDP

338. RTKWK'A SERTOSP OS RTK
NOYYVK EX RTK WEGY ZIR CKVVEM
ARWOLKA GSY YKGY GWNGYOVVEA.
                    —FON TOPTREMKW

339. Z XAZLE ISUIVS AKBS XAS
ZQIWSTTZUL XAKX ASWS ZL IWZLRSXUL
GS GUL'X YU UFXTZHS GZXAUFX
KVVZYKXUWT UL UFW TAZWXT XU
IWUXSRX FT. —PKWPKWK PUYYT TZYQFLH

340. FAJPJ UO RJMJP JRQNBA FUEJ,
NRDJOO ZQN'PJ OJPMURB UF.
                    —EWDGQDE CQPVJO

341. H KDRDQSWZN WF H ADSFMO
UGM UMSCF GHSY HRR GWF RWLD ZM
QDKMXD UDRR-COMUO; ZGDO UDHSF
YHSC PRHFFDF ZM HTMWY QDWOP
SDKMPOWJDY.   —LSDY HRRDO

342. FDLWU N AJDDLD JO AQ CLEIU,
NOX J'A IESSLIUX VL KUV IUYUO
QUNDI FNX PERW, FEV AQ PNZQUD
VCJOWI CU RNO KUV AU HJYU.
                    —IVUSCUO ZDJKCV

343. UNANQPBPSD MYB FESQNR UMYU
FNSFAN CPAA ASSJ YU YDGUMPDL
EYUMNE UMYD NYIM SUMNE.
                    —YDD AYDRNEB

344. SMEF QPY MEDG VGLPKG CR FMG
WUCLG QPY WECA FP HGF SMEF QPY
YRGA FP SEJF. —KCHJPJ KLZEYHMZCJ

345. RDC'I GSSDH CD HZNPRDW DC
IAZ VADCZ OCSZWW NI'W EGXNSF
   —XGXG AGPVZP, "XGXG'W EGXNSF"

76

346. BADAUITTW MYAIZKDB, FSA
YEEUAU YAUMED MGLLAUM VSAUA SA
VKDFAUM.   —JUID TAPEVKFN

347. A FWIJ GID'LY NYYW RPZZAYE CI CVY
XPRY JIRPW KIZ XASCG-WAWY GYPZX.
CVPC AX RPZLYQIDX. AC RDXC NY LYZG
AWYSUYWXALY.   —TIVWWG OPZXIW

348. U TUQ EKZNI KG BV U AINLHPDUL
XPUB U LNIZVSG TINUOQVXL KG BV UL
UDNIKHUL. NZNIFVLN PUG PUQ VLN ULQ
NZNIFVLN XULBG BV BUEO UTVSB KB.
                      —UIB TSHPXUEQ

349. SI GUO BTJ JU CT H VTHQQG CSB
DTHWQSATV, GUO DHKT JU CT
EVTEHVTW IUV ETUEQT JDVUPSAB
CUJJQTF HJ GUO SA JDT ASBDJ.
                      —YSRM XHBBTV

350. XBWN BA RW LTVBXT KQSTZNW
PBZY LTABST OT IQFT WNBKKTG LTMZY
VIMPGSTZ.   —XMYZBZ XVPQRYIPMZ

351. AHIITUOCC? H KWWP NTKHB, H
KWWP FOHR, H KWWP NTKHB HUP H
KWWP GWFHU—WB H YHP GWFHU; TL
POIOUPC WU AWG FXNA AHIITUOCC
MWX NHU AHUPRO.   —KOWBKO YXBUC

352. HDZ WJRT-HZKV NMMJVVJQNHUJR
HDNH CKJHZMHY VNKKUNTZ NRQ
JHDZK YOMD KZWNHUJRYDUCY UY...
AJKTZHAOWRZYY.   —NWUMZ FNWSZK

353. EGJZAVAH UPOY IPOLJ QIVGJ
UPOY EIVGWYJA ZYJ LNVGG HYPQVAH
VL GVXJ LIPMJGVAH NIJ QZGX SJDPYJ
VN LNPFL LAPQVAH. —FIUGGVL WVGGJY

354. QKINI'R RF AMSK GPHRQJS JC
QKJR SMPQMNI QKHQ TJCBP PIFGHNE
RVJC JR WISFAJCD HC ICEHCDINIE
RBCQKIQJS.   —PJPB QFAPJC

355. HGQV GK MH FUV DVJGQBLE WIV
QVL ZV ZFLWVY WG QFUUP.

                   —ETGUBF HWVBLVQ

356. OFJNHS JWRK IH JNFJ VO V

HBHS IHJ F RFKG VQ F KSHUU RVZH

GWXSU, V IXUJ RWWZ NHS UJSFVPNJ

VQ JNH HGHU.　　—YSVQAH ANFSRHU

357. OPOGEM QGLZGOE ST EXG

QSHPEPZPUOB WPJG EXG SEXGL EGO

QGLZGOE U KUV LGQREUEPSO.

　　　　　　　　—XGOLM U. NPBBPOWGL

358. R DRS KRS IP KRJJPN YBXLJPUU

OM LP IHDIU R KHBSXYC XH HIJOEOHS. R

GHDRS KRS IP KRJJPN YBXLJPUU OM ULP

ZBXU CHB HS LHJN. —WJHYOR UXPOSPD

359. TYIAS TOO, FRTI PV T

CAHAVISPTE? RA PV T LTE FRM RTV

IFM QTSV—MEA UAPEN HSPWAE UZ RPV

FPYA, IRA MIRAS UZ MEA MY RPV

QRPOHSAE.　　　　—SMUASI USTHUBSZ

360. ULHW BXTHXWH BJWCB LJB XUW

RFMJBHB, LH MYUMNB CHDB DLH

DZWH DXX LJCL.　　—TMFN L. UMYVFJR

79

361. DVWD'O YVG DVXG HWEX

DZHZAAZY—OZ YX EZQ'D VWBX DZ EZ

XBXAGDVCQU DZEWG.

   —KXDDG LZQXO, "KWAQWKG LZQXO"

362. VRUQHDRFK VU RT UQJUAVAQAK

XTH D ITTE DZDHL USUAKL DRE D

AMKZNK-IDQIK UYTAIQR. —NVRFKRA

VUJKFBV, "FDIRKS DRE ZDFKS."

363. JSFMF'G Y MQRF, H JSHIL. KTQ

ZFJ ASYJ KTQ AYIJ HI RHUF, PQJ ITJ

KTQM GFXTIO XSTHXF, JTT.

             —YRHGTI RQMHF

364. ZP'M MQ SFJRPZBRWWH

JUUJECFV QE PKF AWJPF—HQR OEQT

MQDFQEF'M BZECFUM KJNF SFFE JWW

QNFU ZP.   —XRWZJ YKZWV

365. MEIM EBKTONBQL ONWLK NOL

XMNW OLNYYZ DEYYLR WML REBSKNTOK.

   —NBBSTBQLO, "YNWL BEIMW XEWM

             RNFER YLWWLOUNB"

366. L SMNNU XZCX ZTPCGLXU ZCV

KJJG "COECGRJO" XM LXV YNJVJGX

VXCXJ MB LGRMPYJXJGRU KJRCTVJ

JEMHTXLMG SMNWV MG XZJ YJXJN

YNLGRLYHJ.   —ACGJ SCQGJN

367. H VMMX OFRIN OHSEXOBMD NWM

POC H VMMX OFRIN GHMND. HN

DMMTD NR TM NWON NWMC OSM

PRBGMSVIX NWHBYD VRS RNWMS

EMREXM NR YR RB.   —ZMOB QMSS

368. PI FMN ERQ SLLJ FMNA WLRH

ZWLQ RUU ROMNY FMN RAL UMCPQB

YWLPAC, PY'C DNCY JMCCPOUL FMN

WRGLQ'Y BARCJLH YWL CPYNRYPMQ.

                          —DLRQ SLAA

369. Q NFDIBEVSSX PZQET JF

AFUFSBNFA SVEWRVWF OFMVRIF BG BRD

AFFN QEEFD EFFA PB MBLNSVQE.

                       —HVEF JVWEFD

81

370. CR'E D LXTQZS ADNR RVDR
NDLCRDM LHSCEVWZSR CE D USTFS
BZRZXKZSR DKDCSER NXCWZ.—DXNVCZ
OHSUZX, "DMM CS RVZ ADWCMJ"

371. V'C UD DQP UNP ZQPXP LWWB
QUT DUGPJ DQP EYUHP WL TPM VJ CA
YVLP. VJ LUHD, V'SP ROTD QUB U
CVXXWX EOD WSPX CA GVDHQPJ
DUFYP.   —XWBJPA BUJNPXLVPYB

372. SOWDW'J KM CDWJWKS. SOWDW'J
MKVP SOW GHHWUGLSW BTSTDW LKU
SOW DWZWKS CLJS.—AWMDAW ZLDVGK

373. XO R JNBH UHYESNRSV
HPHNVEOH SRO WH BGGHN SMRQQ
ROU MXPH XO SEOOHSJXSBJ.
                    —MXQR WXNOWRSC

374. PG PAKGB JAB'R IEWG RAA KQID
EMAQR VGRRUBV AQW OUIRQWGX AB
KABGL EX FABV EX PG IEB VGR AQW
DEBJX AB UR. —UNL MESGW OWUGXR

82

375. ZV NAZP DFP FGIBNAWWG, NAR
WXBJ ZHMCWYRHRXN PAR SWIBG
GRNRSN ZX ARC PZNIFNZWX DFP NAFN
XWD PAR SWIBG RFN GRPPRCN
DZNAWIN RFNZXQ ARC YRQRNFKBRP.

—BZPF FBNARC

376. TG KTG V MKF FK FXKQVR
GBDRKL; DE DF TVRL'F EKY XDQ, TG'B
WG TVFHXDLI FGMGODRDKL WP
HVLBMGMDIXF.   —QDMFKL WGYMG

377. XZ MXZQ XK L CTIM TZ
VDQHHXQK, IDLY LB X ETXGO XG YDQ
SXYK?   —QHBL CTBCQVF

378. SIRKPY SMKNKR OD RIV K
VFCOLKP CIPOVOLOKR UMLKJDM AM
YIMDR'V XRIZ AIZ VI POM, LAMKV,
KRY DVMKP. AM KPZKFD AKY KR
KNMRV BIS VAKV.   —UIU AICM

379. IPE AGD'W GUMGIJ XP OI
CBTCVW PTHDHPD. G WEVYCI, HQ IPE
GJY G WEVYCI, JZPEUK OC JWEQQCK
MHWZ XVGJJZPTTCVJ, XVHW, GDK
MPVLJ.   —"AZGDXHDX WHLCJ"

380. IHDD OKWRJKCM NRDD WR IYGN
VHSC KZ G IKTDC IR DHFR HS IYRTR
OKWRJKCM CTROORC PU DHVR G JGN
QRNO GDD WM UTROO?

                —NYR XKVRT, "JGNWGS"

381. ML'A BDAMBJ LI ZMSX D
LJDQBFMST PIUKDSMIS LYDS LI TBL
JMX IZ ISB.   —KBT HJDPOBS

382. RU RGFSMA EHK H TGGC
AMBAMHFOGJHV BGGI, ZWF ESHF KSM
ZHKOBHVVU ZMVOMXMC HZGWF
BGGIOJT EHK FSHF ON UGW EGAIMC
SHAC HJC QAGKQMAMC, KGRMGJM
MVKM EGWVC CG OF NGA UGW.

                —JGAH MQSAGJ

84

383. QEX SWCJ VQLHXV WS YLD LJX

RDSLDFA, FERIPEWWP, LPWIXVFXDFX,

LDP WOVWIXVFXDFX. —LJQ IRDBIXQQXJ

384. VIFIX XNTYI JHOX MNVZ BH JHOX

RMTAZXIV—TB AINFIY JHOX WTZYIRBTHV

OVGXHBIRBIZ.   —XHLIXB HXLIV

385. GR LBC ZDEJ JB UPPJ EPZ

FPBFWP, FGTY CF JVP ZMBES SBWR

QDWW.   —DEBELUBCI

386. R PQWCU XNSVWFN VZJV JSQS,

PZQ PFQVN TQ BJSG EQNBT PRVZQWV

TRMSRSM VZNB, PJT QOVNS J PQBJS.

                —XRFMRSRJ PQQCO

387. IWTGT VGT IWGTT IWRCSH NDJ

ZDC'I STI DKTG RC V WJGGN—ADHRCS

V LDBVC, TVIRCS V PVZ EDHHJB, VCZ

TVIRCS V SDDZ EDHHJB.

                —PTVJ AV PVGGT,

        "LTAUDBT PVUQ, QDIITG."

388. OSZZCUVNN CN OSMCUX S KSEXV,
KPMCUX, JSECUX, JKPNV-WUCG DSACKR
CU SUPGOVE JCGR. —XVPEXV FQEUN

389. W IBFP JH PTFEP QFJJWKQ HSPFT
OFYEIBF W JDHIQDJ W XHISP KHJ OF
EOSF JH PH ESS JDF JDWKQB W
XEKJFP JH PH, OIJ KHX JDEJ W EC
HSPFT, W VWKP JDEJ W PHK'J XEKJ
JH PH JDFC. —KEKYN EBJHT

390. UMOUKP LQWLB U PWBUQZL
GSWLM BSSC OYWG LJWBLCL
XUHWYSQ, LPDLXYUMMK SQL OYWG U
PUCHBUY OUBBYSB YQ YW.

   —WGSCUP CUZQHC, "CUZQHC, D.Y."

391. R SHDI IDINUWSRYJ YCX R SHQ
WXIYWU UIHNE HJC—IBZIAW YCX RW'E
HFF FCXIN. —JUAEU NCEI FII

392. G HAR BARPGB' OHOGBWR COBEGBK.
GR'W LJALDJ G MOB'R WROBK.

   —OQMPGJ NYBEJQ, "ODD GB RPJ IOCGDZ"

86

393. CPMMZPFI ZV DEA CIMIGU
VXPMZDF AXI BIAALJJZDI, SLA VXPMZDF
AXI SLMNID EB BZDNZDF AXI
BIAALJJZDI MIVAPLMPDA ZD AXI
BZMVA HGPJI.   —JPGWZD AMZGGZD

394. UABUFO UWXCRBAPZEP U SUIAJ
SYUCXAF. JDQO BQAA JDYRB JDROP
QC WDUYEP RSS EIUYZ UCZ EQHP FRI
JDP RLLRYJICQJF JR WRKKQJ KRYP.
                    —KUYX JBUQC

395. YG VQYTS VYQ ZVASI GNVA
VQYTSI, BMSX EMSNS KVSI LFLJ VYQ
ZVAS GNVA?   —HFXS EFPXSN

396. VES YUS VEMUR M OY UYV LFUV
VY JS BFXXSO MD KMTDV XFOI. MV
DYNUOD XMGS F DFOOXS EYTDS.
                    —PFBZNSXMUS GSUUSOI

87

397. D KNA'H HCDAR XCJ BFHCSGY
PFUS HCSB. NPP LNLDSY TF DY PSNR
NH LFHC SATY.

        —LDYCFO TFIEPNY QSNUSG

398. HC GNSSOJ ZCU CXL N GCSZOJ
QT, TZO UNSFZOT ZOJ GQLLXO-NPO
FZQXLJOH KCJ TQPHT CK
QGBJCEOGOHS.

        —KXCJQLN TFCSS-GNVUOXX

399. KEKC PDZVS, JKAA-OIDGUYP-GT
KCUANFY UNIAF VIK PVGUYP OS
PYKNI XDPYKIF PD ODNA VAA
EKUUNKF WDI VP AKVFP V XDCPY VCZ
V YVAW, QGFP NC MVFK DCK DW PYK
ZNCCKI UGKFPF PGICF GT JNPYDGP
YNF PKKPY.   —MVAENC PINAANC

400. AX J CXSO, FMNNMQN MQ AKL
KJSF NSXHQF MI OXSL SLGJDMQN
AKJQ NXMQN VMIKMQN. —JQXQUOXHI

Clue One

This section offers a single clue, or letter equivalent, for each puzzle. If Z = A in cryptogram number one, then Z will equal A throughout that puzzle. Since each puzzle has its own code, the clue and letter equivalents will be different in each cryptogram.

1. N = P	32. O = F	63. M = R	94. U = D
2. N = F	33. X = L	64. T = W	95. C = W
3. B = R	34. X = M	65. T = V	96. E = U
4. X = T	35. Z = Y	66. Y = M	97. W = G
5. D = B	36. Y = H	67. W = L	98. C = F
6. O = T	37. M = P	68. M = T	99. J = G
7. C = J	38. M = Y	69. U = C	100. G = U
8. O = V	39. P = L	70. F = Q	101. V = C
9. E = W	40. P = U	71. D = W	102. T = B
10. A = F	41. D = P	72. G = F	103. F = N
11. Q = M	42. L = U	73. X = G	104. O = T
12. F = D	43. G = B	74. H = F	105. P = G
13. F = D	44. P = L	75. Z = C	106. G = M
14. V = R	45. G = M	76. Q = M	107. K = B
15. Q = F	46. K = S	77. R = S	108. E = N
16. A = L	47. Z = N	78. G = N	109. M = L
17. M = F	48. J = M	79. B = C	110. A = R
18. I = F	49. J = N	80. N = B	111. N = H
19. B = L	50. P = M	81. F = B	112. D = F
20. E = D	51. N = O	82. U = G	113. Z = M
21. H = G	52. K = T	83. S = N	114. Y = J
22. H = T	53. D = N	84. U = D	115. O = F
23. D = H	54. S = D	85. D = P	116. A = T
24. L = S	55. J = R	86. Q = B	117. P = S
25. K = B	56. S = F	87. P = V	118. T = Y
26. K = N	57. C = M	88. D = C	119. E = S
27. P = S	58. R = W	89. S = M	120. U = P
28. M = G	59. L = P	90. G = T	121. C = D
29. W = O	60. B = H	91. V = D	122. K = H
30. F = P	61. K = C	92. S = B	123. G = M
31. Y = V	62. J = N	93. W = T	124. L = R

125. A = B	165. R = O	205. U = N	245. Q = O
126. E = M	166. J = D	206. I = D	246. S = G
127. V = T	167. A = T	207. Y = K	247. O = N
128. C = H	168. S = R	208. F = G	248. K = V
129. Z = M	169. P = B	209. W = G	249. C = D
130. J = M	170. R = O	210. X = K	250. P = F
131. P = Y	171. U = Y	211. U = M	251. W = N
132. B = G	172. W = T	212. H = C	252. A = O
133. I = B	173. E = P	213. K = P	253. L = D
134. K = D	174. Q = F	214. Y = M	254. L = M
135. Q = L	175. U = L	215. Z = C	255. N = W
136. T = P	176. B = R	216. Q = C	256. O = F
137. F = P	177. D = W	217. T = N	257. F = R
138. X = G	178. V = A	218. W = B	258. K = M
139. J = Y	179. N = M	219. X = U	259. Q = W
140. K = B	180. U = R	220. C = M	260. W = M
141. T = X	181. R = W	221. Q = D	261. Y = G
142. L = A	182. B = U	222. Z = F	262. K = F
143. R = N	183. N = H	223. H = N	263. Y = C
144. E = T	184. E = M	224. D = F	264. Q = S
145. B = Y	185. C = R	225. X = H	265. S = Y
146. V = N	186. J = L	226. A = R	266. J = Y
147. B = V	187. B = G	227. E = S	267. F = R
148. D = T	188. O = T	228. N = M	268. N = K
149. K = R	189. A = L	229. Y = D	269. L = B
150. V = R	190. Z = S	230. A = F	270. M = N
151. O = N	191. O = P	231. V = N	271. I = D
152. B = R	192. Y = M	232. I = V	272. G = D
153. A = N	193. I = T	233. Y = L	273. G = N
154. Y = X	194. S = D	234. A = D	274. G = T
155. X = L	195. H = M	235. T = D	275. S = T
156. R = U	196. M = T	236. F = D	276. T = M
157. A = M	197. K = M	237. E = O	277. V = N
158. B = M	198. W = G	238. B = R	278. Y = C
159. N = R	199. U = W	239. D = Y	279. W = N
160. L = R	200. L = H	240. D = S	280. M = O
161. S = F	201. F = B	241. F = W	281. X = W
162. M = Y	202. Y = L	242. K = P	282. D = P
163. I = M	203. L = N	243. Q = I	283. E = D
164. L = Y	204. Z = J	244. R = N	284. L = M

285. T = F	314. C = E	343. F = P	372. D = R
286. B = G	315. O = Y	344. S = W	373. S = C
287. Y = J	316. D = T	345. S = L	374. P = W
288. Y = S	317. T = N	346. S = H	375. V = F
289. U = T	318. U = D	347. L = V	376. M = L
290. E = V	319. T = N	348. X = W	377. B = M
291. F = M	320. M = D	349. B = G	378. U = B
292. Q = B	321. B = D	350. A = F	379. U = L
293. S = R	322. H = B	351. P = D	380. W = M
294. I = U	323. I = D	352. H = T	381. M = I
295. B = W	324. A = H	353. G = L	382. Z = B
296. K = P	325. A = P	354. C = N	383. J = R
297. U = C	326. D = M	355. H = S	384. B = T
298. Q = N	327. E = Y	356. G = Y	385. L = Y
299. H = T	328. D = W	357. O = N	386. P = W
300. A = R	329. Q = G	358. D = M	387. B = M
301. J = N	330. E = M	359. R = H	388. O = H
302. H = G	331. O = S	360. U = W	389. P = D
303. G = L	332. V = T	361. O = S	390. C = M
304. Z = C	333. M = C	362. U = S	391. X = W
305. I = G	334. F = C	363. G = S	392. L = P
306. D = S	335. E = R	364. S = B	393. G = L
307. T = S	336. Q = L	365. B = N	394. S = F
308. W = N	337. X = C	366. E = V	395. A = M
309. Q = M	338. N = M	367. E = P	396. B = C
310. V = T	339. Y = G	368. G = V	397. L = B
311. O = R	340. P = R	369. N = P	398. T = S
312. K = D	341. R = L	370. J = Y	399. I = R
313. G = B	342. F = B	371. L = F	400. N = G

Clue Two

This section offers a second clue, or letter equivalent, for each puzzle. If M = T in cryptogram number one, then M will equal T throughout that puzzle. Since each puzzle has its own code, the clue and letter equivalents will be different for each cryptogram.

1. Q = N	32. J = V	63. G = M	94. B = W
2. W = L	33. L = Y	64. W = B	95. Y = B
3. W = Y	34. R = P	65. H = N	96. I = L
4. L = M	35. V = L	66. A = N	97. J = B
5. A = D	36. A = K	67. C = N	98. M = Y
6. R = C	37. R = W	68. A = B	99. K = F
7. N = M	38. C = S	69. S = B	100. I = P
8. J = M	39. F = G	70. H = M	101. X = G
9. H = B	40. F = C	71. T = C	102. Z = C
10. B = Q	41. X = M	72. Y = V	103. N = F
11. A = F	42. F = P	73. B = W	104. L = S
12. B = C	43. M = Z	74. R = M	105. O = W
13. V = B	44. H = S	75. S = P	106. V = F
14. O = B	45. I = L	76. M = R	107. M = Z
15. Y = C	46. Q = G	77. A = P	108. F = X
16. S = G	47. I = T	78. E = T	109. V = Y
17. A = P	48. H = D	79. Q = J	110. U = W
18. O = L	49. M = B	80. C = P	111. T = C
19. M = D	50. H = F	81. Y = K	112. A = D
20. I = P	51. J = L	82. T = P	113. W = F
21. Z = S	52. F = C	83. B = P	114. U = G
22. M = J	53. F = K	84. L = N	115. D = B
23. G = N	54. Z = G	85. V = O	116. R = C
24. G = N	55. M = H	86. M = F	117. M = G
25. E = C	56. M = H	87. L = C	118. Y = D
26. M = P	57. Z = C	88. B = M	119. B = P
27. W = L	58. L = M	89. U = B	120. P = L
28. W = B	59. U = M	90. N = B	121. G = V
29. T = M	60. W = P	91. X = B	122. D = S
30. M = N	61. M = D	92. H = D	123. K = C
31. I = C	62. K = M	93. T = M	124. Z = M

125. Q = J	165. N = J	205. R = S	245. A = G
126. D = B	166. R = M	206. M = G	246. D = B
127. Z = H	167. M = P	207. H = B	247. J = F
128. J = P	168. U = F	208. Q = L	248. O = M
129. H = Y	169. L = M	209. T = K	249. T = L
130. W = K	170. G = Z	210. V = G	250. T = P
131. R = M	171. I = M	211. W = P	251. L = P
132. H = M	172. J = G	212. W = T	252. H = G
133. X = L	173. Y = F	213. J = M	253. S = F
134. B = W	174. D = N	214. H = B	254. T = F
135. Y = K	175. D = B	215. J = V	255. J = N
136. O = K	176. J = P	216. Y = G	256. C = Y
137. K = G	177. E = V	217. B = G	257. Q = L
138. V = D	178. F = T	218. S = L	258. U = W
139. P = R	179. K = G	219. F = C	259. C = L
140. B = W	180. X = B	220. Z = R	260. Y = L
141. Y = W	181. V = K	221. N = S	261. F = M
142. D = G	182. C = F	222. W = B	262. E = W
143. C = J	183. R = D	223. A = H	263. U = S
144. I = M	184. B = Y	224. O = G	264. H = M
145. N = J	185. A = P	225. D = M	265. F = V
146. N = L	186. Y = P	226. H = D	266. M = G
147. V = K	187. Z = M	227. I = P	267. G = M
148. H = N	188. W = L	228. K = L	268. G = W
149. N = P	189. H = S	229. I = S	269. A = V
150. S = J	190. U = C	230. F = J	270. O = P
151. D = G	191. E = W	231. Q = R	271. Z = Y
152. S = W	192. U = D	232. C = R	272. Z = G
153. R = A	193. X = H	233. J = M	273. V = S
154. A = M	194. G = P	234. Z = M	274. E = V
155. I = B	195. M = D	235. Y = M	275. X = D
156. B = C	196. F = B	236. X = H	276. Y = T
157. T = B	197. N = T	237. L = H	277. M = G
158. A = C	198. P = O	238. P = D	278. H = P
159. Z = H	199. J = M	239. T = P	279. Q = C
160. Q = T	200. W = C	240. X = C	280. C = W
161. Q = M	201. E = G	241. U = P	281. M = B
162. H = C	202. N = M	242. C = M	282. Q = B
163. B = H	203. M = X	243. M = S	283. F = T
164. V = B	204. W = S	244. Y = H	284. S = D

285. V = G	314. L = G	343. L = G	372. C = P
286. E = W	315. M = B	344. Z = L	373. O = N
287. K = W	316. O = D	345. I = T	374. O = P
288. Z = M	317. J = K	346. Y = P	375. P = S
289. R = L	318. A = L	347. R = M	376. T = W
290. W = F	319. M = L	348. Z = V	377. E = D
291. L = G	320. I = Z	349. E = P	378. N = G
292. B = M	321. J = Y	350. Y = G	379. X = G
293. N = K	322. Y = U	351. I = P	380. O = S
294. O = C	323. N = B	352. Y = S	381. T = G
295. C = Z	324. S = C	353. H = G	382. U = Y
296. L = C	325. K = R	354. G = P	383. F = C
297. G = B	326. M = X	355. E = G	384. Z = D
298. E = Y	327. Y = P	356. Y = P	385. F = P
299. B = P	328. A = P	357. Q = P	386. O = F
300. H = G	329. M = C	358. Y = R	387. E = P
301. U = Y	330. U = T	359. U = B	388. W = K
302. W = L	331. H = C	360. L = H	389. J = B
303. Y = W	332. O = M	361. K = B	390. O = W
304. C = F	333. N = M	362. S = Y	391. B = X
305. B = M	334. W = M	363. J = T	392. C = M
306. N = W	335. P = B	364. W = L	393. F = G
307. A = T	336. T = P	365. O = R	394. J = T
308. Q = R	337. K = N	366. R = C	395. L = B
309. H = Y	338. Y = D	367. P = W	396. K = F
310. K = C	339. V = L	368. A = R	397. T = D
311. H = C	340. V = B	369. M = C	398. H = N
312. J = R	341. U = W	370. L = P	399. U = G
313. W = P	342. P = L	371. G = K	400. O =M

Solutions

1. When we talk to God, we're praying. When God talks to us, we're schizophrenic. —Jane Wagner

2. This is a free country. Folks have a right to send me letters, and I have a right not to read them. —William Faulkner

3. Never invest your money in anything that eats or needs repairing. —Billy Rose

4. Once the toothpaste is out of the tube, it's hard to get it back in. —H.R. Haldeman

5. The biggest seller is cookbooks and the second is diet books— how not to eat what you've just learned how to cook. —Andy Rooney

6. There is no dilemma compared with that of the deep-sea diver who hears the message from the ship above, "Come up at once. We are sinking." —Robert Cooper

7. Age is strictly a case of mind over matter. If you don't mind, it doesn't matter. —Jack Benny

8. The real menace in dealing with a five-year-old is that in no time at all you begin to sound like a five-year-old. —Jean Kerr

9. Many a man owes his success to his first wife and his second to his success. —Jim Backus

10. It's no longer a question of staying healthy. It's a question of finding a sickness you like. —Jackie Mason

11. I have a microwave fireplace. You can lay down in front of the fire all night in eight minutes. —Stephen Wright

12. How can you be expected to govern a country that has two hundred forty-six kinds of cheese? —Charles de Gaulle

13. When the burdens of the presidency seem unusually heavy, I always remind myself it could be worse. I could be a mayor. —Lyndon B. Johnson

14. We don't have any refrigerators. We have a few potbelly stoves, but they're on the coaching staff.   —Coach Dave Currey

15. Disney, of course, has the best casting. If he doesn't like an actor, he just tears him up.   —Alfred Hitchcock

16. Having a family is like having a bowling alley installed in your brain.   —Martin Mull

17. There are no sick people in North Oxford. They are either dead or alive. It's sometimes difficult to tell the difference, that's all.   —Barbara Pym

18. When a man of forty falls in love with a girl of twenty, it isn't her youth he is seeking but his own.   —Lenore Coffee

19. The great corrupter of public man is the ego...Looking at the mirror distracts one's attention from the problem.

—Dean Acheson

20. Nothing is impossible for the man who doesn't have to do it himself.   —Anonymous

21. My ignorance of science is such that if anyone mentioned copper nitrate, I should think he was talking about policemen's overtime.   —Archbishop Frederick Donald Coggan

22. Never drink black coffee at lunch; it will keep you awake in the afternoon.   —Jilly Cooper

23. Nolan Ryan is pitching a lot better now that he has his curve ball straightened out.   —Joe Garagiola

24. Sex in the hands of public educators is not a pretty thing.
—Kevin Arnold, "The Wonder Years"

25. Getting kicked out of the American Bar Association is like getting kicked out of the Book-of-the-Month Club.

—Melvin Belli

26. Once the trust goes out of a relationship, it's really no fun lying to 'em anymore.   —Norm Peterson, "Cheers"

27. Always remember that we pass this way but once. Unless your spouse is reading the road map.   —Robert Orben

28. At one point, Howard, we were hunters and gatherers and then seems like all of a sudden we became partygoers.
                                                      —Jane Wagner

29. The feminist movement has helped open minds and kitchens to the notion that men can be at home on the range.
                                                      —René Veaux

30. Politics: the gentle art of getting votes from the poor and campaign funds from the rich, by promising to protect each from the other.   —Anonymous

31. A vegetarian is a person who won't eat anything that can have children.   —David Brenner

32. After a year in therapy, my psychiatrist said to me, "Maybe life isn't for everyone."   —Larry Brown

33. The secret of staying young is to live honestly, eat slowly, and lie about your age.   —Lucille Ball

34. There is a fine difference of perspective between getting involved and being committed. In ham and eggs, the chicken is involved, but the pig is committed.   —John-Allen Price

35. I buried a lot of my ironing in the back yard. —Phyllis Diller

36. A diplomat is a person who can tell you to go to hell in such a way that you actually look forward to the trip.
                                                      —Cassie Stinnett

37. It's not that I'm afraid to die. I just don't want to be there when it happens.   —Woody Allen

38. As far as I'm concerned, the only reason for cooking is to keep your hands busy while you think about something else.
                                                      —Sue Grafton

39. Life, in my estimation, is a biological misadventure that we terminate on the shoulders of six strange men whose only objective is to make a hole in one with you.   —Fred Allen

40. You can trust a crystal ball about as far as you can throw it.
—Faith Popcorn

41. People with honorary awards are looked upon with disfavor. Would you let an honorary mechanic fix your brand-new Mercedes?
—Neil Simon

42. If you shoot a mime, should you use a silencer?
—Stephen Wright

43. When I'm alone, I can sleep crossways in bed without an argument.
—Zsa Zsa Gabor

44. The man with six kids will always be happier than the man with six million dollars, because the man with six million dollars always wants more.
—Anonymous

45. If I had as many affairs as they say, I would now be speaking to you from inside a jar at the Harvard Medical School.
—Frank Sinatra

46. She got her good looks from her father. He's a plastic surgeon.
—Groucho Marx

47. The shortest distance between two points is under construction.
—Noelie Alioto

48. Intelligence is when you find a mistake in your boss's work. Wisdom is when you think about it and decide not to mention it.
—Anonymous

49. We are all born charming, fresh, and spontaneous and must be civilized before we are fit to participate in society.
—Judith Martin

50. I have my faults, but being wrong ain't one of them.
—Jimmy Hoffa

51. The truth does not change according to our ability to stomach it emotionally.
—Flannery O'Connor

52. Life was a lot simpler when what we honored was father and mother rather than all major credit cards.
—Robert Orben

53. I'm tired of all this nonsense about beauty being only skin-deep. That's deep enough. What do you want, an adorable pancreas?
—Jean Kerr

54. One of the things I've discovered in general about raising kids is that they really don't give a damn if you walked five miles to school.
—Patty Duke

55. The trouble with some women is that they get all excited about nothing and then marry him.
—Cher

56. I figure if high heels were so wonderful, men would be wearing them.
—Sue Grafton

57. If most auto accidents happen within five miles of home, why don't we move ten miles away?
—Michael Davis

58. Why do they call it the rush hour when nothing moves?
—Mork, "Mork and Mindy"

59. People are broad-minded. They'll accept the fact that a person can be an alcoholic, a dope fiend, a wife beater and even a newspaperman, but if a man doesn't drive, there's something wrong with him.
—Art Buchwald

60. The thing that impresses me most about America is the way parents obey their children.
—Edward, Duke of Windsor

61. No day is so bad it can't be fixed with a nap.
—Carrie Snow

62. The brain is an organ that starts working the moment you get up in the morning and does not stop until you get into the office.
—Robert Frost

63. I have no problem with the rich, only with those who have a problem being rich.
—David Brown

64. This used to be a government of checks and balances. Now it's all checks and no balances.
—Gracie Allen

65. Whenever I'm asked what kind of writing is the most lucrative, I have to say, ransom notes.
—H.N. Swanson

66. I must say I hate money, but it's the lack of it I hate most.

—Katherine Mansfield

67. As Miss America, my goal is to bring peace to the world and then to get my own apartment.

—Jay Leno

68. If you have to learn it from a self-help book, you may be beyond help.

—Wes Smith

69. When I was born, I was so surprised I couldn't talk for a year and a half.

—Gracie Allen

70. There is no question that Rumanian-Jewish food is heavy... One meal is equal in heaviness, I would guess, to eight or nine years of steady mung-bean eating.

—Calvin Trillin

71. The only time a woman really succeeds in changing a man is when he's a baby.

—Natalie Wood

72. Television has done much for psychiatry by spreading information about it, as well as contributing to the need for it.

—Alfred Hitchcock

73. Going into a supermarket without a list is the surest way to buy everything but what you went in for in the first place.

—Helen Nash

74. Can you imagine a world without men? No crime and lots of happy fat women.

—Marion Smith

75. We'd all like a reputation for generosity, and we'd all like to buy it cheap.

—Mignon McLaughlin

76. Never lend your car to anyone to whom you have given birth.

—Erma Bombeck

77. As we say in the sewer, if you're not prepared to go all the way, don't put your boots on in the first place.

—Ed Norton, "The Honeymooners"

78. There must be more to life than just eating and getting bigger.

—Trina Paulus

79. A coward dies a hundred deaths, a brave man only once...But then, once is enough, isn't it?
—Judge Harry Stone, "Night Court"

80. If pregnancy were a book, they would cut the last two chapters. —Nora Ephron

81. The Rose Bowl is the only one I've ever seen that I didn't have to clean. —Erma Bombeck

82. I was always taught to respect my elders and I've now reached the age when I don't have anybody to respect.
—George Burns

83. One night I stayed up all night playing poker with tarot cards. I got a full house and four people died. —Stephen Wright

84. You need that guy like a giraffe needs strep throat.
—Ann Landers

85. If I didn't start painting, I would have raised chickens.
—Grandma Moses

86. My boyfriend and I broke up. He wanted to get married, and I didn't want him to. —Rita Rudner

87. Maybe the answer to selective service is to start everyone off in the army and draft them for civilian life as needed.
—Bill Vaughn

88. Mike Hammer drinks beer and not cognac because I can't spell cognac. —Mickey Spillane

89. He reminds me of the man who murdered both his parents, and then, when his sentence was about to be pronounced, pleaded for mercy on the grounds that he was an orphan.
—Abraham Lincoln

90. The next best thing to being clever is being able to quote someone who is. —Mary Pettibone Poole

91. The human mind treats a new idea the way the body treats a strange protein; it rejects it. —P.B. Medawar

92. A politician ought to be born a foundling and remain a bachelor.
—Lady Bird Johnson

93. Tennis is like marrying for money. Love has nothing to do with it.
—Phyllis Diller

94. When you are down and out something always turns up—and it is usually the noses of your friends.
—Orson Welles

95. If at first you don't succeed, try, try again. Then quit. No sense being a damn fool about it.
—W.C. Fields

96. A study of economics usually reveals that the best time to buy anything is last year.
—Marty Allen

97. Too bad all the people who know how to run the country are busy driving taxicabs and cutting hair.
—George Burns

98. Research tells us that fourteen out of any ten individuals like chocolate.
—Sandra Boynton

99. It's not easy being a mother. If it were, fathers would do it.
—Dorothy, "The Golden Girls"

100. I quit school in the fifth grade because of pneumonia. Not because I had it, but because I couldn't spell it.
—Rocky Graziano

101. Don't accept rides from strange men, and remember that all men are strange.
—Robin Morgan

102. I have a seashell collection; maybe you've seen it? I keep it on beaches all over the world.
—Stephen Wright

103. Like my old skeenball coach used to say, "Find out what you don't do well, then don't do it."
—Alf, "Alf"

104. I'm throwing twice as hard as I ever did. The ball's just not getting there as fast.
—Lefty Gomez

105. Just be considerate, accept each other for what you are, and don't point out the fact that the hair he's losing on his head is now growing out of his nose—and his ears.
—Peg Bundy, "Married with Children"

106. I love getting mail—just the fact that someone licked a stamp for you is very reassuring.

—Thomas Magnum, "Magnum P.I."

107. We were both in love with him...I fell out of love with him, but he didn't.

—Zsa Zsa Gabor

108. I was an excellent student until ten, and then my mind began to wander.

—Grace Paley

109. Blessed are the young, for they shall inherit the national debt.

—Herbert Hoover

110. I know how to do anything—I'm a mom.   —Roseanne Barr

111. Never allow your child to call you by your first name. He hasn't known you long enough.

—Fran Lebowitz

112. Someone did a study of the three most-often-heard phrases in New York City. One is "Hey, taxi." Two is "What train do I take to Bloomingdale's?" And three is "Don't worry, it's only a flesh wound."

—David Letterman

113. The three-martini lunch is the epitome of American efficiency. Where else can you get an earful, a bellyful, and a snootful at the same time?

—Gerald R. Ford

114. Your sons weren't made to like you. That's what grandchildren are for.

—Jane Smiley

115. No diet will remove all the fat from your body because the brain is entirely fat. Without a brain you might look good, but all you could do is run for public office.

—Covert Bailey

116. The young always have the same problem—how to rebel and conform at the same time. They have solved this by defying their parents and copying one another.

—Quentin Crisp

117. If you love the law and you love good sausage, don't watch either of them being made.

—Betty Talmadge

118. Women never have young minds. They are born three thousand years old.

—Shelagh Delaney

119. Contrary to popular opinion, the hustle is not a new dance step—it is an old business procedure. —Fran Lebowitz

120. A paranoid is a man who knows a little of what's going on. —William Burroughs

121. If it wasn't for Philo T. Farnsworth, inventor of television, we'd still be eating frozen radio dinners. —Johnny Carson

122. The average, healthy, well-adjusted adult gets up at seven-thirty in the morning feeling just plain terrible. —Jean Kerr

123. Asthma doesn't seem to bother me any more unless I'm around cigars or dogs. The thing that would bother me most would be a dog smoking a cigar. —Steve Allen

124. I have found the best way to give advice to your children is to find out what they want and then advise them to do it. —Harry S Truman

125. I figure if the kids are alive at the end of the day, I've done my job. —Roseanne Barr

126. There are more pleasant things to do than beat up people. —Muhammad Ali

127. After all, what is reality anyway? Nothin' but a collective hunch. —Jane Wagner

128. More people will die from hit-or-miss eating than from hit-and-run driving. —Duncan Hines

129. You know what makes this country great? You don't have to be witty or clever, as long as you can hire someone who is. —Ted Baxter, "The Mary Tyler Moore Show"

130. America is a large, friendly dog in a very small room. Every time it wags its tail, it knocks over a chair. —Arnold Toynbee

131. I don't want any "yes-men" around me. I want everybody to tell me the truth even if it costs them their jobs. —Samuel Goldwyn

132. I started out with nothing. I still have most of it.
—Michael Davis

133. Things may come to those who wait, but only the things left by those who hustle. —Abraham Lincoln

134. Remember Ginger Rogers did everything Fred Astaire did, but she did it backwards and in high heels. —Faith Whittlesey

135. When you become senile, you won't know it. —Bill Cosby

136. I am one of those people who just can't help getting a kick out of life—even when it's a kick in the teeth. —Polly Adler

137. A hospital bed is a parked taxi with the meter running.
—Groucho Marx

138. Dealing with network executives is like being nibbled to death by ducks. —Eric Sevareid

139. My problem lies in reconciling my gross habits with my net income. —Errol Flynn

140. Asked why he robbed banks, the notorious American bank robber Willie Sutton is reputed to have remarked, "Because that's where the money is." —Theodore H. White

141. It's relaxing to go out with my ex-wife because she already knows I'm an idiot. —Thomas Warren

142. We're all born brave, trusting, and greedy, and most of us remain greedy. —Mignon McLaughlin

143. In department stores, so much kitchen equipment is bought indiscriminately by people who just come in for men's underwear. —Julia Child

144. Love is like the measles. The older you get it, the worse the attack. —Mary Roberts Rinehart

145. Just learn your lines and don't bump into the furniture.
—Spencer Tracy

146. I have gained and lost the same ten pounds so many times over and over again my cellulite must have deja vu.

—Jane Wagner

147. I've been rich and I've been poor. Believe me, honey, rich is better. —Sophie Tucker

148. There are no atheists on turbulent airplanes. —Erica Jong

149. Just remember, once you're over the hill you begin to pick up speed. —Charles Schulz

150. There are times not to flirt. When you're sick. When you're with children. When you're on the witness stand. —Joyce Jillson

151. When men reach their sixties and retire, they go to pieces. Women go right on cooking. —Gail Sheehy

152. A woman who will tell her age will tell anything.

—Rita Mae Brown

153. It isn't necessary to be rich and famous to be happy. It's only necessary to be rich. —Alan Alda

154. You can become about as exciting as your food blender. The kids come in, look you in the eye, and ask if anybody's home.

—Erma Bombeck

155. I'm at an age when my back goes out more than I do.

—Phyllis Diller

156. A worried man could borrow a lot of trouble with practically no collateral. —Helen Nielsen

157. I'm devoting my life to being a psychiatric patient. It's a vocation, like being a nun, only a lot more expensive.

—Joyce Rebeta-Burditt

158. Why am I bothering to eat this chocolate? I might as well just apply it directly to my thighs.

—Rhoda Morgenstern, "The Mary Tyler Moore Show"

159. Yeah, I read history. But it doesn't make you nice. Hitler read history, too. —Joan Rivers

160. Remember that as a teenager you are at the last stage in your life when you will be happy to hear that the phone is for you   —Fran Lebowitz

161. To fall in love with yourself is the first secret of happiness. Then if you're not a good mixer, you can always fall back on your own company.   —Robert Morley

162. A male gynecologist is like an auto mechanic who has never owned a car.   —Carrie Snow

163. Americans no longer experience vacations. They simply Sony them so they can ignore them for the rest of the year.
                                                            —John Grisham

164. You don't have to be dowdy to be a Christian.
                                                    —Tammy Faye Bakker

165. Only two things are necessary to keep one's wife happy. One is to let her think she is having her own way, and the other, to let her have it.   —Lyndon B. Johnson

166. When I was a kid my parents moved a lot—but I always found them.   —Rodney Dangerfield

167. I think on-stage nudity is disgusting, shameful, and damaging to all things American. But if I were twenty-two with a great body, it would be artistic, tasteful, patriotic, and a progressive religious experience.   —Shelley Winters

168. Never go to a doctor whose office plants are dead.
                                                            —Erma Bombeck

169. After thirty, a body has a mind of its own.   —Bette Midler

170. Too often travel, instead of broadening the mind, merely lengthens the conversation.   —Elizabeth Drew

171. All them surgeons—they're highway robbers. Why do you think they wear masks when they work on you?
                                —Archie Bunker, "All in the Family"

172. As for butter versus margarine, I trust cows more than chemists.   —Joan Gussow

173. If the people don't want to come out to the park, nobody's gonna stop them. —Yogi Berra

174. One of the funny things about the stock market is that every time one person buys, another sells, and both think they are astute. —Anonymous

175. Old people shouldn't eat health foods. They need all the preservatives they can get. —Robert Orben

176. The more you read about politics, the more you got to admit that each party is worse than the other. —Will Rogers

177. It's a rare person who wants to hear what he doesn't want to hear. —Dick Cavett

178. I always wanted to get into politics, but I was never light enough to make the team. —Art Buchwald

179. Life with Mary was like being in a telephone booth with an open umbrella—no matter which way you turned, you got it in the eye. —Jean Kerr

180. You and I come by road or rail, but economists travel on infrastructure. —Margaret Thatcher

181. I don't care what is written about me so long as it isn't true. —Katharine Hepburn

182. People who fight fire with fire usually end up with ashes. —Abigail Van Buren

183. Man does not live by words alone, despite the fact that sometimes he has to eat them. —Adlai E. Stevenson

184. Education is a wonderful thing. If you couldn't sign your name, you'd have to pay cash. —Rita Mae Brown

185. I think of birth as the search for a larger apartment. —Rita Mae Brown

186. I like long walks, especially when they are taken by people who annoy me. —Fred Allen

187. The best executive is the one who has sense enough to pick good men to do what he wants done, and self-restraint enough to keep from meddling with them while they do it.
—Theodore Roosevelt

188. I always have a quotation for everything—it saves original thinking.   —Dorothy L. Sayers

189. The true snob never rests; there is always a higher goal to attain, and there are, by the same token, always more and more people to look down upon.   —Russell Lynes

190. If men had to have babies, they would only ever have one each.   —Princess Diana

191. You can't expect to hit the jackpot if you don't put a few nickels in the machine.   —Flip Wilson

192. I lost everything in the post-natal depression.
—Erma Bombeck

193. I told 'em the truth and they fell for it.
—Judge Harry Stone, "Night Court"

194. An artist is somebody who produces things that people don't need to have.   —Andy Warhol

195. When my mother had to get dinner for eight, she'd just make enough for sixteen and only serve half.   —Gracie Allen

196. His body's taken on the weight his mind still refuses to accept.   —Toni Cade Bambara

197. A committee is a group that keeps minutes and loses hours.
—Milton Berle

198. Politics is the art of looking for trouble, finding it everywhere, diagnosing it incorrectly, and applying the wrong remedies.   —Groucho Marx

199. As we say in the sewer, time and tide wait for no man.
—Ed Norton, "The Honeymooners"

200. Please understand the reason why Chinese vegetables taste so good. It is simple. The Chinese do not cook them, they just threaten them!
—Jeff Smith

201. There is a fine line between fishing and standing on the bank like an idiot.
—Anonymous

202. The illegal we do immediately. The unconstitutional takes a little longer.
—Henry A. Kissinger

203. A woman in love will do almost anything for a man, except give up the desire to improve him.
—Nathaniel Branden

204. If there was any justice in this world, oil company executive bathrooms would smell like the ones in their gas stations.
—Johnny Carson

205. We can't all be heroes because somebody has to sit on the curb and clap as they go by.
—Will Rogers

206. Middle age is when you're faced with two temptations and you choose the one that will get you home by nine o'clock.
—Ronald Reagan

207. If I had known I was going to live this long, I'd have taken better care of myself.
—Eubie Blake

208. One way to get high blood pressure is to go mountain climbing over molehills.
—Earl Wilson

209. That would be a good thing for them to cut on my tombstone: wherever she went, including here, it was against her better judgment.
—Dorothy Parker

210. If the cat has kittens in the oven, that don't make 'em biscuits.
—Elisabeth Ogilvie

211. Business is a good game—lots of competition and a minimum of rules. You keep score with money.
—Nolan Bushnell

212. Having a baby is like taking your lower lip and forcing it over your head.
—Carol Burnett

213. Being popular is important. Otherwise people might not like you. —Mimi Pond

214. Somewhere on this globe every ten seconds, there is a woman giving birth to a child. She must be found and stopped.
—Sam Levenson

215. There's three moments in a man's life: when he buys a house, a car, and a new color TV. That's what America is all about. —Archie Bunker, "All in the Family"

216. Football is not a contact sport. It's a collision sport. Dancing is a good example of a contact sport. —Duffy Daugherty

217. My wife is a light eater...As soon as it's light, she starts to eat. —Henny Youngman

218. The disparity between a restaurant's price and food quality rises in direct proportion to the size of the pepper mill.
—Bryan Miller

219. You know, if you shoot me, you'll lose a lot of these humanitarian awards. —Chevy Chase, "Fletch"

220. Show me a man who doesn't make mistakes and I'll show you a man who doesn't do anything. —Theodore Roosevelt

221. I've developed a new philosophy—I only dread one day at a time. —Charles Schulz

222. My wife and I tried two or three times in the last forty years to have breakfast together, but it was so disagreeable we had to stop. —Winston Churchill

223. I once wanted to be an atheist, but I gave up—they have no holidays. —Henny Youngman

224. All I ever needed to know I learned in kindergarten. Don't hit people. Clean up your own mess. —Robert Fulghum

225. Adorable children are considered to be the general property of the human race. Rude children belong to their mothers.
—Judith Martin

226. It's not true I had nothing on. I had the radio on.
—Marilyn Monroe

227. The penalty of success is to be bored by people who used to snub you. —Nancy Astor

228. I have a wonderful make-up crew. They're the same people restoring the Statue of Liberty. —Bob Hope

229. When they call the roll in the Senate, the senators do not know whether to answer "Present" or "Not guilty."
—Theodore Roosevelt

230. Manhattan is a narrow island off the coast of New Jersey devoted to the pursuit of lunch. —Raymond Sokolov

231. Trust your husband, adore your husband, and get as much as you can in your own name. —Joan Rivers

232. I never eat in a restaurant that's over a hundred feet off the ground and won't stand still. —Calvin Trillin

233. Laugh and the world laughs with you, snore and you sleep alone. —Mrs. Patrick Campbell

234. God don't make no mistakes—that's how He got to be God.
—Archie Bunker, "All in the Family"

235. I might not know how to use thirty-four words where three would do, but that does not mean I don't know what I'm talking about. —Ruth Shays

236. I hate when my foot falls asleep during the day because I know it's going to be up all night. —Stephen Wright

237. For three days after death, hair and fingernails continue to grow, but phone calls taper off. —Johnny Carson

238. I never panic when I get lost. I just change where I want to go. —Rita Rudner

239. Any man who goes to a psychiatrist ought to have his head examined. —Samuel Goldwyn

240. I love you no matter what you do, but do you have to do so much of it? —Jean Illsley-Clarke

241. It's a small world, but I wouldn't want to paint it.
—Stephen Wright

242. Many people who imagine they are live wires are only shocking. —Mary Pettibone Poole

243. A woman does not break into your house and clean it for fun. —Rick Simon, "Simon and Simon"

244. Ronald Reagan has held the two most demeaning jobs in the country—president of the United States and radio broadcaster of the Chicago Cubs. —George Will

245. It's wonderful to be married to an archaeologist—the older you get, the more interested he is in you. —Agatha Christie

246. Standing in the middle of the road is very dangerous; you get knocked down by the traffic from both sides.
—Margaret Thatcher

247. I am also five three and in the neighborhood of one thirty. It is a neighborhood I would like to get out of. —Flannery O'Connor

248. It's not true that life is one damn thing after another—it's one damn thing over and over. —Edna St. Vincent Millay

249. I've run more risk eating my way across the country than in all my driving. —Duncan Hines

250. I'm very old-fashioned. I believe that people should stay married for life, like pigeons and Catholics. —Woody Allen

251. Having been unpopular in high school is not just cause for book publication. —Fran Lebowitz

252. There are far too many men in politics and not enough elsewhere. —Hermione Gingold

253. In short, the best thing to do is behave in a manner befitting one's age. If you are sixteen or under, try not to go bald.
—Woody Allen

254. It's not the men in my life that counts, it's the life in my men. —Mae West

255. An idealist is one who, on noticing that a rose smells better than a cabbage, concludes that it will also make better soup.
—H.L. Mencken

256. I prefer the Chinese method of eating...You can do anything at the table except arm wrestle. —Jeff Smith

257. I have a simple philosophy. Fill what's empty. Empty what's full. Scratch where it itches. —Alice Roosevelt Longworth

258. Like women all over America, my mother confronted tragedy and death with cold ham and Jell-O salad.
—Kevin Arnold, "The Wonder Years"

259. Whenever someone asks me if I want water with my scotch, I say I'm thirsty, not dirty. —Joe E. Lewis

260. When you live alone, you can be sure that the person who squeezed the toothpaste tube in the middle wasn't committing a hostile act. —Ellen Goodman

261. It has begun to occur to me that life is a stage I'm going through. —Ellen Goodman

262. Short-term amnesia is not the worst affliction if you have an Irish flair for the sauce. —Norman Mailer

263. Next week there can't be any crisis. My schedule is already full. —Henry A. Kissinger

264. The monarchy is so extraordinarily useful. When Britain wins a battle, she shouts, "God save the queen"; when she loses, she votes down the prime minister. —Winston Churchill

265. Don't worry about avoiding temptation. As you grow older, it will avoid you. —Joey Adams

266. Dogs come when they're called; cats take messages and get back to you. —Mary Bly

267. I think kangaroos have a good deal. I like that pouch setup. I'd have a baby if it would mature in a handbag.   —Rita Rudner

268. Infinity, it could be time on an ego trip for all I know.
—Jane Wagner

269. When a man sits with a pretty girl for an hour, it seems like a minute. But let him sit on a hot stove for a minute—and it's longer than any hour. That's relativity.   —Albert Einstein

270. She was in perfect condition except for one thing—she was dead.   —Quincy, "Quincy"

271. Childhood is that wonderful time when all you need to do to lose weight is bathe.   —Anonymous

272. Carmine and I have an understanding. I'm allowed to date other men, and he's allowed to date ugly women.
—Laverne, "Laverne and Shirley"

273. Neurotic means he is not as sensible as I am, and psychotic means that he is even worse than my brother-in-law.
—Karl Menninger

274. It is while trying to get everything straight in my head that I get confused.   —Mary Virginia Micka

275. There's no such thing as a sure thing. That's why they call it gambling.   —Oscar Madison, "The Odd Couple"

276. "Maintenance-free" usually means that when it breaks, it can't be fixed.   —Anonymous

277. Anybody who has any doubt of the ingenuity or the resourcefulness of a plumber never got a bill from one.
—George Meany

278. Next week I have to take my college aptitude test. In my high school, they didn't even teach aptitude.
—Tony Banta, "Taxi"

279. Most people do not consider dawn to be an attractive experience—unless they are still up.   —Ellen Goodman

280. A few years ago it was considered chic to serve beef Wellington; fortunately, like Napoleon, it met its Waterloo.

—René Veaux

281. There has always been a food processor in the kitchen. But once upon a time she was usually called the missus, or Mom.

—Sue Berkman

282. I am rather like a mosquito in a nudist camp; I know what I ought to do, but I don't know where to begin.   —Stephen Bayne

283. I think we consider too much the good luck of the early bird, and not enough of the bad luck of the early worm.

—Franklin D. Roosevelt

284. If you never want to see a man again, say, "I love you. I want to marry you. I want to have your children." They leave skid marks.   —Rita Rudner

285. You can lead a herring to water, but you have to walk really fast or they die.   —Rose Nylund, "The Golden Girls"

286. If criminals wanted to grind justice to a halt, they could do it by banding together and all pleading not guilty.

—Dorothy Wright Wilson

287. I went on a diet, swore off drinking and heavy eating, and in fourteen days I had lost exactly two weeks.   —Joe E. Lewis

288. Stay humble. Always answer the phone—no matter who else is in the car.   —Jack Lemmon

289. An incompetent attorney can delay a trial for years or months. A competent attorney can delay one even longer.

—Evelle J. Younger

290. The thing I enjoyed most were visits from children. They did not want public office.   —Herbert Hoover

291. My mother always used to say: "The older you get, the better you get—unless you're a banana."

—Rose Nylund, "The Golden Girls"

292. I believe that if ever I had to practice cannibalism, I might manage if there were enough tarragon around.   —James Beard

293. I'd like to be lucky enough so that I could throw the soap away after the letters are worn off.   —Andy Rooney

294. When everyone is out to get you, paranoia is only good thinking.   —Johnny Fever, "WKRP Cincinnati"

295. We become adolescents when the words that adults exchange with one another become intelligible to us.

—Natalia Ginzberg

296. Bankruptcy is a legal proceeding in which you put your money in your pants pocket and give your coat to your creditors.   —Joey Adams

297. Claustrophobia? It's a dreadful fear of Santa Claus.
—Vinnie Barbarino, "Welcome Back, Kotter"

298. One of the glories of New York is its ethnic food, and only McDonald's and Burger King equalize us all.   —John Corry

299. Time has little to do with infinity or jelly doughnuts.
—Thomas Magnum, "Magnum, P.I."

300. If everyone is thinking alike, then somebody isn't thinking.
—General George Patton

301. I'm going to my psychoanalyst one more year, then I'm going to Lourdes.   —Woody Allen

302. Good breeding consists in concealing how much we think of ourselves and how little we think of the other person.
—Mark Twain

303. The trouble with the rat race is that even if you win, you're still a rat.   —Lily Tomlin

304. A pate is nothing more than a French meat loaf that's had a couple cocktails.   —Carol Cutler

305. Insanity is doing the same thing over and over again, but expecting different results.   —Rita Mae Brown

306. Six years and you haven't learned anything—it's white wine with Hershey bars.   —Harvey Barros, "Making the Grade"

307. To be good is noble, but to teach others to be good is even nobler—and less trouble.   —Mark Twain

308. My definition of a redundancy is an airbag in a politician's car.   —Larry Hagman

309. Money can't buy happiness, but it will get you a better class of memories.   —Ronald Reagan

310. Conscience: an inner voice that warns us that somebody is looking.   —H.L. Mencken

311. Who wears the pants in this house? I do, and I also wash and iron them.   —Dennis Thatcher

312. Fall is my favorite season in Los Angeles, watching the birds change colors and fall from the trees.   —David Letterman

313. I had to face the facts, I was pear-shaped. I was a bit depressed because I hate pears.   —Charlotte Bingham

314. Some films could only have been cast in one way: Screen tests were given and the losers got the parts.   —Gene Shalit

315. One man was so mad at me that he ended his letter: Beware. You will never get out of this world alive.

—John Steinbeck

316. Sometimes a person has to go a very long distance out of his way to come back a short distance correctly.

—Edward Albee

317. You gotta know the rules before you can break 'em. Otherwise, it's just no fun.   —Sonny Crockett, "Miami Vice"

318. The difference between life and the movies is that a script has to make sense and life doesn't.   —Joseph L. Mankiewicz

319. An intellectual is someone who can listen to the *William Tell Overture* and not think of the Lone Ranger.   —Anonymous

320. The most wasteful "brain drain" in America today is the drain in the kitchen sink. —Elizabeth Gould Davis

321. "Extra" money is defined as that which you have in your possession just before the car breaks down. —Anonymous

322. Suburbia is where the developer bulldozes out the trees, then names the streets after them. —Bill Vaughn

323. People do think that if they avoid the truth, it might change to something better before they have to hear it.
—Marsha Norman

324. A pessimist is someone who can look at the land of milk and honey and see only calories and cholesterol. —Anonymous

325. If the human body recognized agony and frustration, people would never run marathons, have babies, or play baseball.
—Carlton Fisk

326. I'm mad that money counts for everything in this world— and that I don't have any. —Alex Reiger, "Taxi"

327. Television is an invention that permits you to be entertained in your living room by people you wouldn't have in your home. —David Frost

328. What we are is our parents' children; what we become is our children's parents. —Merrit Malloy

329. The nice thing about being a celebrity is that when you bore people, they think it's their fault. —Henry A. Kissinger

330. About the time we can make the ends meet, somebody moves the ends. —Herbert Hoover

331. I'm the candidate who forgot to take off her hat before she threw it in the ring. —Gracie Allen

332. Death and taxes and childbirth! There's never any convenient time for any of them! —Margaret Mitchell

333. A fanatic is one who can't change his mind and won't change the subject. —Winston Churchill

334. I don't want to achieve immortality through my work, I want to achieve immortality by not dying.   —Woody Allen

335. True love comes quietly, without banners or flashing lights. If you hear bells, get your ears checked.   —Erich Segal

336. Lots of women buy just as many wigs and makeup things as I do. They just don't wear them all at the same time.

—Dolly Parton

337. The cocktail party remains a vital Washington institution, the official intelligence system.   —Barbara Howar

338. There's nothing in the middle of the road but yellow stripes and dead armadillos.   —Jim Hightower

339. I think people have the impression that here in Princeton we won't go outside without alligators on our shirts to protect us.   —Barbara Boggs Sigmund

340. There is never enough time, unless you're serving it.

—Malcolm Forbes

341. A celebrity is a person who works hard all his life to become well-known, then wears dark glasses to avoid being recognized.   —Fred Allen

342. Broke a mirror in my house, and I'm supposed to get seven years bad luck, but my lawyer thinks he can get me five.

—Stephen Wright

343. Television has proved that people will look at anything rather than each other.   —Ann Landers

344. What you have become is the price you paid to get what you used to want.   —Mignon McLaughlin

345. Don't allow no weirdos on the phone unless it's family.

—Mama Harper, "Mama's Family"

346. Generally speaking, the poorer person summers where he winters.   —Fran Lebowitz

347. I know you've been married to the same woman for sixty-nine years. That is marvelous. It must be very inexpensive.
—Johnny Carson

348. A bad liver is to a Frenchman what a nervous breakdown is to an American. Everyone has had one and everyone wants to talk about it. —Art Buchwald

349. If you get to be a really big headliner, you have to be prepared for people throwing bottles at you in the night.
—Mick Jagger

350. Most of us become parents long before we have stopped being children. —Mignon McLaughlin

351. Happiness? A good cigar, a good meal, a good cigar and a good woman—or a bad woman; it depends on how much happiness you can handle. —George Burns

352. The long-term accommodation that protects marriage and other such relationships is...forgetfulness. —Alice Walker

353. Cleaning your house while your children are still growing is like shoveling the walk before it stops snowing.
—Phyllis Diller

354. There's so much plastic in this culture that vinyl leopard skin is becoming an endangered synthetic. —Lily Tomlin

355. Some of us are becoming the men we wanted to marry.
—Gloria Steinem

356. Father told me that if I ever met a lady in a dress like yours, I must look her straight in the eyes. —Prince Charles

357. Ninety percent of the politicians give the other ten percent a bad reputation. —Henry A. Kissinger

358. A man can be called ruthless if he bombs a country to oblivion. A woman can be called ruthless if she puts you on hold.
—Gloria Steinem

359. After all, what is a pedestrian? He is a man who has two cars—one being driven by his wife, the other by one of his children.
—Robert Bradbury

360. When someone sings his own praises, he always gets the tune too high.
—Mary H. Waldrip

361. That's why they made tomorrow—so we don't have to do everything today.
—Betty Jones, "Barnaby Jones"

362. Insurance is no substitute for a good alarm system and a twelve-gauge shotgun.
—Vincent Isbecki, "Cagney and Lacey"

363. There's a rule, I think. You get what you want in life, but not your second choice, too.
—Alison Lurie

364. It's so beautifully arranged on the plate—you know someone's fingers have been all over it.
—Julia Child

365. High insurance rates are what really killed the dinosaurs.
—Announcer, "Late Night with David Letterman"

366. I worry that humanity has been "advanced" to its present state of incompetency because evolution works on the Peter Principle.
—Jane Wagner

367. I feel about airplanes the way I feel about diets. It seems to me that they are wonderful things for other people to go on.
—Jean Kerr

368. If you can keep your head when all about you are losing theirs, it's just possible you haven't grasped the situation.
—Jean Kerr

369. I personally think we developed language because of our deep inner need to complain.
—Jane Wagner

370. It's a proven fact that capital punishment is a known detergent against crime.
—Archie Bunker, "All in the Family"

371. I'm at the age where food has taken the place of sex in my life. In fact, I've just had a mirror put over my kitchen table.
—Rodney Dangerfield

372. There's no present. There's only the immediate future and the recent past. —George Carlin

373. In a true democracy everyone can be upper class and live in Connecticut. —Lisa Birnbach

374. We women don't care too much about getting our pictures on money as long as we can get our hands on it.
—Ivy Baker Priest

375. If this was adulthood, the only improvement she could detect in her situation was that now she could eat dessert without eating her vegetables. —Lisa Alther

376. We owe a lot to Thomas Edison: If it wasn't for him, we'd be watching television by candlelight. —Milton Berle

377. If life is a bowl of cherries, what am I doing in the pits?
—Erma Bombeck

378. Ronald Reagan is not a typical politician because he doesn't know how to lie, cheat, and steal. He always had an agent for that. —Bob Hope

379. You can't always go by expert opinion. A turkey, if you ask a turkey, should be stuffed with grasshoppers, grit, and worms.
—"Changing Times"

380. Will somebody tell me what kind of a world we live in where somebody dressed up like a bat gets all my press?
—The Joker, "Batman"

381. It's easier to find a traveling companion than to get rid of one. —Peg Bracken

382. My mother was a good recreational cook, but what she basically believed about cooking was that if you worked hard and prospered, someone else would do it for you.
—Nora Ephron

383. The four stages of man are infancy, childhood, adolescence, and obsolescence. —Art Linkletter

384. Never raise your hand to your children—it leaves your midsection unprotected. —Robert Orben

385. If you want to meet new people, pick up the wrong golf ball. —Anonymous

386. I would venture that Anon, who wrote so many poems without signing them, was often a woman. —Virginia Woolf

387. There are three things you don't get over in a hurry—losing a woman, eating a bad possum, and eating a good possum. —Beau la Barre, "Welcome Back, Kotter"

388. Happiness is having a large, loving, caring, close-knit family in another city. —George Burns

389. I used to dread getting older because I thought I would not be able to do all the things I wanted to do, but now that I am older, I find that I don't want to do them. —Nancy Astor

390. Always enter a strange hotel room with extreme caution, especially one with a samurai warrior in it. —Thomas Magnum, "Magnum, P.I."

391. I have everything now I had twenty years ago—except now it's all lower. —Gypsy Rose Lee

392. I got nothin' against mankind. It's people I can't stand. —Archie Bunker, "All in the Family"

393. Marriage is not merely sharing the fettuccine, but sharing the burden of finding the fettuccine restaurant in the first place. —Calvin Trillin

394. Always acknowledge a fault frankly. This will throw those in charge off guard and give you the opportunity to commit more. —Mark Twain

395. If olive oil comes from olives, then where does baby oil come from? —Jane Wagner

396. The one thing I do not want to be called is First Lady. It sounds like a saddle horse. —Jacqueline Kennedy

397. I can't think why mothers love them. All babies do is leak at both ends.   —Bishop Douglas Feaver

398. No matter how old a mother is, she watches her middle-age children for signs of improvement.   —Florida Scott-Maxwell

399. Even today, well-brought-up English girls are taught by their mothers to boil all veggies for at least a month and a half, just in case one of the dinner guests turns up without his teeth.
                                                                         —Calvin Trillin

400. To a worm, digging in the hard ground is more relaxing than going fishing.   —Anonymous

Index

127